Pass the Jelly

Tales of Ordinary Enlightenment

A MEMOIR

Gary Crowley

SENTIENT PUBLICATIONS

First Sentient Publications edition 2009

A paperback original

Cover design by Kim Johansen, Black Dog Design
Book design by Timm Bryson

Library of Congress Cataloging-in-Publication Data
Crowley, Gary.
  Pass the jelly : tales of ordinary enlightenment : a memoir / Gary
Crowley.
     p. cm.
  ISBN 978-1-59181-092-6
  1. Life. I. Title.
  BD431.C875 2009
  158.1—dc22
                                    2009021325

Printed in the United States of America
10 9 8 7 6 5 4 3 2 1

SENTIENT PUBLICATIONS
A Limited Liability Company
1113 Spruce Street
Boulder, CO 80302
www.sentientpublications.com

PASS THE JELLY

CONTENTS

NOTE TO READERS

This book is a memoir. Thus, everything in it is absolutely true, except for the stuff that isn't. Certain people and events are compilations, and some names have been changed. Rest assured, the core and essence of these laugh-out-loud wisdom tales are intact.

Pass the Jelly

A long chain of cause and effect had led to my being where I was, and while this is true for everyone all the time, I knew it wasn't personal. It never is. And knowing this allowed me to soak in the entire spectacle.

I happened to be sitting on the divider between the buzzing north- and southbound lanes of Interstate 5, California's busiest freeway. The first rain of the season had come the night before. It brings back to life the dormant oil in the roads, and the freshly greased pavement becomes akin to the black ice I grew up with in New England. The water, the oil, and the hydroplaning cars had made me one of the inevitable accident statistics of the day.

The sun hammered against the morning drizzle as I sat and watched drivers race past me. It was inspiring. Despite the wrecks of cars that lined their route, these drivers were still willing to flirt with the razor-sharp edge of Newton's unforgiving laws of motion. I found myself impressed, as I often am, by the unflinching optimism of the human spirit.

To my left, my freshly crumpled car was being raised into the air by a tow truck. I'd already done the ritualistic exchange of insurance information with the woman who had helped make my accident possible. She was perfectly nice, but we both knew our time together was fleeting. Although brief, our relationship was intense and memorable, which is more than many people share. When she merged back into her regular life, as I knew she must, it seemed predestined.

The requisite stocky-cop-with-a-mustache had already come and gone. The first rain was his busiest day of the year, so my experiencing of him as a stoic, heavily armed cliché was all he had time for. I'm sure by the end of his work day I would no doubt be filed deep in his memory banks as another forgettable motorist. All things considered, our mutually uneventful experience was probably a good thing when it comes to encounters with law enforcement.

With a wave of his hand, the tow truck driver signaled to me that it was time for us to go. I walked over and stepped into the passenger side of the truck.

"Where to?" asked the driver, with the name Jim on his light blue shirt.

"Well, Jim," I said, "I'm not really sure."

"Name's not Jim. Jim quit. His shirt fit."

His words were spoken in a kind but indifferent manner that I found oddly refreshing. I waited for his true identity to be revealed, but nothing came. He wasn't giving me much to work with, and technically he did say his name was not Jim, so Not Jim was what I went with.

"I guess we should bring the car to an auto body shop. Then the insurance company can decide what they want to do with it," I stumbled.

"Yep," said Not Jim.

"Do you know any reputable shops in the area?"

"Nope."

I realized Not Jim required a bit more precision than your average Not Joe.

"Do you have any friends who own auto body shops in the area?" I asked.

"Dave's Auto Body is about seven miles away. He's as good as any other."

"That'd be great," I confirmed.

Those were the last words Not Jim and I spoke on our ride. For the next seven miles we sat in some of the most comfortable silence I've ever experienced.

I must admit that I was intrigued by *the way* of Not Jim. Everybody has *a way*, but Not Jim had that little something extra you don't run into every day. Once he caught my attention, I was fascinated. I forgot all about my recently compacted vehicle destined for the crusher. I was now fully present with my driver.

I noticed that Not Jim gripped the steering wheel in a way that was relaxed, but also precise. You can tell a lot about a person from their hands, and he had the hands of a poet. Don't get me wrong— they weren't delicate by any means, but you could tell they had a sensitivity that allowed him to meet each task with the exact amount of tension or force required. No more, no less.

Not Jim was the type who shook your hand and matched the firmness of your grip perfectly. He didn't give you the dead fish handshake of someone who is not going to be present with you, nor was he the vice grip kind of guy who was there to impose himself on others. Not Jim was my kind of guy. He was a modern-day wrangler out rescuing humanity's strays on their daily cattle drive to and from work. He was over the drama of it all, and his calmness helped his passengers realize the obvious fact that car accidents are just part of life.

During our drive I realized what a deep spiritual practice being a tow truck driver could be. For someone so inclined, it would be impossible not to gain a profound perspective on life. Day after day you show up at scenes where, only moments earlier, fates of life and death had been dealt. You would be intimately involved with the sleek, new cars that had been crushed into accordion-like sculptures. Even simple scenes of people leaning against a broken-down vehicle would continually reinforce the futility of resisting *what is.*

For a man with the hands of a poet, driving a wrecker would probably not be a bad way to go. Not Jim's workday carried the repeating lesson that life gives us each a full range of experiences, whether we like it or not.

This understanding certainly wasn't new. The first dramatic portrayal of life's wide experiential range was delivered to me in my youth in the form of a live theatrical performance. It was given by my friend Dan's Uncle Bernie, who chauffeured him to and from school. Uncle Bernie's van had the name and phone number of his school for the performing arts painted on its side, along with the two masks from ancient Greek theatre. You know—one mask crying, the other mask laughing.

I knew Dan's Uncle Bernie was a man of many talents because not only did he run an acting school, he also planned weddings and did interior design for the rich people in Providence, Rhode Island. He was also "a really good dresser," as my mom often noted. But even as a child I was aware that his choice in clothing was about more than just his keen fashion sense. It reflected a meticulousness in his nature that was woven into the very fabric of his life.

One day I was walking out of school and spotted Uncle Bernie waiting for his nephew. As usual, he was leaning against his van with a lit cigarette propped between the relaxed index and middle fingers of his right hand. When on call, both the cigarette and his hand hovered in the vicinity of his right ear, so that the slightest desire for nicotine would release his wrist and spin the cigarette down and around to the front of his mouth for an effortless drag of burning tobacco. Inside the school, Dan was busy pleading his innocence for the crime of placing a thumbtack on Brian O'Connell's seat earlier that day, so he was going to be a while. Knowing Uncle Bernie had some time on his hands, I stopped in front of his van and pointed at the two masks.

"What do those masks mean?" I asked.

I'm pretty sure Uncle Bernie was a method actor because he didn't just deliver a line to his audience (me) and move on. He took on an entirely new persona for the sole purpose of imparting his message through the perfect vehicle. First, his thumb and index finger clamped down on his cigarette and pressed it against his now taut lips. Then his cheeks puckered as he drew long and hard on the wisdom deep within him. He exhaled a slow stream of smoke as he assessed my ability to handle the piercing truth he was about to deliver, and his steely gaze locked my attention in place. At this point, even I was aware that he had transformed from his normal persona into Marlon Brando.

"You're born. You die. In between, you laugh, you cry," he said with a palpable indifference.

I'm sure he could have let go with Shakespeare's *Seven Ages of Man*, but he went with the concise answer, which I appreciated. "You're born. You die. In between, you laugh, you cry" were the only words he said. He then stepped on his cigarette butt and climbed into his van without giving me another look. Uncle Bernie's concise summary of the experience of living has stuck with me to this day.

Over the years I've come to see that this lesson is not just in ancient Greek theater. The Sumerians were talking about it in their garden of paradise story way back in 3500 B.C. The Christians, Persians, Greeks, Tibetans, and American Indians have the lesson in their garden stories as well. The exile from the garden occurs because the "tree of knowledge" gives us the concept of duality, of opposites: life and death, male and female, good and evil, pleasure and pain, joy and sorrow.

Without knowledge we are innocent, but we are also ignorant. All the garden stories, as well as the masks from Greek theatre, tell us that the duality of life is everywhere, all the time. That's what living *in time* is—experiencing opposites. If you fight the play of opposites that make up life, you suffer. It's not that complicated. It's not rocket science or brain surgery. Let's face it, it's not even rocket surgery.

Not Jim pulled into the parking lot of the auto body shop. He backed my car between two other wrecks with only inches to spare on each side. We both stepped out of his truck and I walked over to watch him work the controls on its side. In under a minute, my car and I were free to go.

"All set," Not Jim reported with a polite nod of his head.

For him it was a rather long-winded diatribe designed to let me know that, while my auto accident might be a big deal for me, it was something that happened all day, every day, so I needn't get too worked up about it. I appreciated his concern and willingness to share his wisdom.

As Not Jim pulled away, his concisely expressed perspective brought to mind another teaching that was imparted to me in my youth. It led to one of my most profound understandings of "the way." I was about twelve years old back in Seekonk, Massachusetts, when it occurred. Let's just say there was a lot of duality to deal with back then, so you had to catch on quickly. Seekonk was a name the Indians (Sitting Bull, not Gandhi) gave my town. It means "black goose." The Indians were the givers of names for many of the lakes, rivers, and towns in New England. They were even kind enough to provide names for many of our ski resorts and country clubs. We were basically taught that the Indians gave Thanksgiving dinner to the Pilgrims, took a little time to teach us their names for things, but then got bored and decided to move closer to all the casinos.

When I was a kid, I used to watch my dad read the newspaper every morning from 7:10 to 7:30 as he ate breakfast before heading off to work. Dad was an Irish Catholic blue-collar guy from Rhode Island. He was a good man whose rules for living were pretty simple: do your best to live the Golden Rule and go to church every Sunday. When it came to politics, he pretty much drank whatever beverage the Democratic Party was serving. In his world, everything the Democrats did was right and everything the Republicans did was wrong.

To this day, I find the true believers out there in the world utterly fascinating. The wonderful thing is that there are always some on both sides of any issue. The efficiency of their decision-making processes is impressive, to say the least. When I'm in their presence, I can't help but think, "Isn't that great." The total commitment they hold to their side being right is often completely unaffected by inconvenient things like facts. This must be why people find politics so interesting.

Each morning when my dad read the newspaper, I would hear him exclaim, "You've gotta be kidding me," or "How could someone do that?" A simple groan of "What?" was also common, but my personal favorite was the occasional, "Unbelievable." "Unbelievable" was usually blurted out in regard to some politician going back on a campaign promise, a union boss caught getting kickbacks, or some similarly outrageous claim like "gravity will be present again today."

My dad kept most of his distress about the world between himself and the newspaper. When it was time to go to work, he declared a temporary truce with reality and went on with his day. I, however, had witnessed Dad's morning routine far too often by the time I was twelve for it to be ignored any longer. It was then that I decided to begin my lifelong journey as a master of the obvious.

The question I was about to ask my dad had been gestating in my little brain for a few months. At first I had only a vague sense of it, but over time it became pretty clear. I knew this was one of those big questions, so I waited until a Sunday morning when Dad wouldn't have to rush out the door to work. I wanted time for us to dialogue about the finer points of not only the question itself, but of the implications that its possible answers might have on all of our lives.

I sat eating my Kellogg's Corn Puffs in my favorite yellow bowl and watched my dad reading the paper. I was waiting for the perfect moment to ask my question. You know, so it didn't seem forced. Then it happened. My dad read that the Democratic mayor of neighboring Providence, one of the nation's most corrupt cities at the time, was about to be sent to jail again.

"Unbelievable," my dad said as he read the headline.

"Dad?" I said, like I was going to ask about fertilizing the lawn, "If you're surprised about the things you read in the newspaper all the time, do you think that maybe you have an inaccurate perception of the way people and things actually are? Not that you aren't going to be surprised about the specifics of events—but in a general sense, do you think you should be so shocked all the time at human beings continually doing the same stuff?"

My dad looked at me as if an apparition of Dan Rather had replaced his loyal son and was blindsiding him in a *60 Minutes* interview. Being a father of five children, my dad instinctively gave my little brother Billy the were-you-in-on-this? look. When my brother's very sincere, big-eyed I-had-absolutely-nothing-to-do-with-this expression passed muster, my dad's eyes returned to me.

With his mouth closed, my dad took in a slow breath. He then made an audible sound by rapidly exhaling through his nostrils. This was an exhale that signaled inconvenience or annoyance, not anger. I would hear it when he picked the wrong sized wrench while working on the car, or when the lawn mower wouldn't start for some unknown reason. It wasn't a good exhale sound, but as far as exhale sounds go, it could have been a lot worse.

An audible exhale through the mouth would have been a sign of anger. It was usually reserved for times when my dad was unexpectedly forced to deal with his children torturing each other. When I was about nine, my sister and I spent approximately forty-five minutes passing a roll of string over and under the bed in which my brother Bill was sleeping. Bill awoke to his mummified condition, and his screams brought Dad sprinting into the room. At that memorable moment, a teeth-clenched, open-mouthed, audible exhale occurred. It did not go unnoticed by my sister, who was wise enough to escape in the commotion. I was left to try and explain how the mummification process was an accident, but my dad just wouldn't listen.

Back at the breakfast table, after a slight pause, Dad's response to my question turned out to be refreshingly cogent, clear, and concise.

"Pass the jelly, please," he ordered.

I waited and I waited and I waited. That was it. "Pass the jelly, please" was his response to my life-altering question.

I realized one of two things had just happened. Either my dad had completely denied a question that would be cyanide to his fundamental perception of reality by dissociating from the entire event and storing it deep in his cranium where it could only be accessed through intense hypnosis with an entire team of psychoanalysts in Vienna, or my dad was a true spiritual master and had given me the deepest answer possible, not through words but through demonstration of the principle he wished to convey.

I was twelve years old and this was my dad, so naturally I chose the latter option. Plus, at the time I had the benefit of a more than slight obsession with the blind Buddhist master on the television show *Kung Fu*. He was always giving Grasshopper esoteric discourses on life. "Pass the jelly, please" was obviously embedded with a deep and profound meaning regarding the nature of existence. The lesson was plain to see if you knew just the right angle from which to view it.

Like the enlightenment experience of the sage that spontaneously occurred at the ringing of a temple bell, all became clear to me as I reached for and passed the jelly (grape, by the way, never strawberry). As I handed my father the jelly, our fingers touched. The principle being demonstrated crystallized in my mind: *People do what they do. That's what they do. And that is it.*

I'm not claiming that this insight made the rest of my life a state of perpetual bliss, but I would be lying if I said it hasn't profoundly affected me. In that moment it seemed like I experienced the world much more "as it is." This insight allowed me to see that everyone, including me, is continually doing what they do—effortlessly. I watched in amazement as my parents, teachers, and friends all continually did what they did. Once I saw the Pass the Jelly Principle, the only question left was how I could have missed it for my entire life, when it was right in front of me all the time.

Don't get me wrong, the seeds of recognition had been germinating in the soil for a few years before my awakening to the principle. One of the first seeds of understanding was planted four years earlier during the famous Georgie Porgie Incident of '73. It was overshadowed a bit by the Watergate Scandal, so I'm not surprised if you missed it.

The Georgie Porgie Incident occurred in Mr. Mendrachowski's third-grade class at Newman Elementary School. For those of you who recall, his classroom was directly across the hall from the hot new teacher, Miss Smutek, and down the hall from Mr. Grasso, who was notorious for beaning his daydreaming students in the head with chalk-filled erasers from across the room.

Anyway, one morning at the end of our science section, Mr. Mendrachowski got us all hyped-up about an experiment we were going to do the following day. He informed us that the experiment would require a standard carpenter's nail and that he needed a volunteer to bring it in. He made it clear: no nail = no experiment. Because we third graders had yet to be too jaded by the world, at least half the class raised their hands to volunteer for the important assignment. Mr. Mendrachowski was obviously an optimist because of all the people in class to rest our scientific fates upon, he chose George. After all, this was the George of "Georgie Porgie pumpkin pie/Kissed a girl and made her cry" fame.

George was a perfectly wonderful kid. He was the universal playmate, the guy who got along well with everyone. We all liked George, but to say he was dependable would be a stretch even a professional contortionist would not attempt. I don't know if he whacked his head on a doorknob when he was four and shut off the dependability center of his brain, but it just wasn't there. And it was obvious to anyone who knew George.

"Okay George, if you don't remember to bring a nail to school tomorrow, then we won't get to have science," Mr. Mendrachowski repeated three times.

George agreed to the deal, but it seemed to me that it was an extreme and unnecessary risk. Science was my favorite subject. If we didn't have science, then we would end up doing more spelling or grammar. Yuck. Only wimps who wanted to be writers liked spelling and grammar. I didn't want to waste time on useless subjects when I needed all the science I could get in order to be an astronaut. Ever since I stood in my neighbor's kitchen on July 21, 1969, I'd wanted to be an astronaut. That was the date I watched Neil Armstrong walk on the moon. Despite seeing it on a fuzzy black-and-white TV screen, it's one of my most vivid childhood memories.

"George," Mr. Mendrachowski said the next day when science was scheduled to begin.

A bright-eyed, but clueless smile was George's only response.

"The nail," our teacher nudged. "Did you remember to bring the nail to school today?"

George slapped his forehead with the palm of his hand and let out an apologetic laugh. The entire class followed with a groan of disappointment. They assumed that the much hyped nail experiment was now not going to take place.

I sat patiently, hoping that my externally optimistic and encouraging teacher also had a realistic perspective on life and would soon produce a nail of his own. After all, my astronaut training was on the line here. But Mr. Mendrachowski did not produce a nail of his own.

"Okay then. No nail, no science class. That was the deal," Mr. Mendrachowski said.

"I brought a nail," I announced, "just in case George forgot."

I can still see the look on Mr. Mendrachowski's face. He looked at me like I was Nostradamus predicting the rise of Hitler, four hundred years before he came to power. I walked up to the front of the class and handed over the nail. He stared down at me with his head tilted to the side and eyebrows contracted with a look that said, "How did you know George would forget?" Either that or it was a look of, "Why you little shit, I was going to use this time to correct papers while you kids worked on spelling exercises."

Regardless of what his look meant, I couldn't believe someone would so blatantly disregard the realities of what so plainly and simply *is*. The day before, upon coming home from school, I had gone directly into the basement and procured a three-inch carpenter's nail from the old mayonnaise jar in the basement. You know, the one right next to the toolbox. I assumed five or six other kids from my class would be doing exactly the same thing, which was my own denial of *what is*. I thought six of us holding up nails for Mr. Mendrachowski the next day might hammer the point home for the entire class. It turns out I was the only one.

The Georgie Porgie Incident of '73 was one of many seeds that were planted along the way, until all at once, through my father's brilliant demonstration of the Pass the Jelly Principle, it became clear to me. At twelve years old, I realized that the entire foundation of modern Western civilization was flawed.

It appeared to me that Western civilization was based on the premise that human beings are rational creatures who make conscious choices about who and how they are. I'd been around for only about twelve years, but my question for people who believed this was, "What color is the sky in your world?" Obviously, it wasn't the same color as the sky above my planet.

Everyone I knew woke up each morning the same basic person they were the night before, without even trying. Mrs. Healy was always the lady who baked cookies for the neighborhood kids. Mr. O'Reilly was always the grumpy guy who didn't like us playing in front of his house. Mrs. Mooney yelled at us every year when we would try to harvest chestnuts from her tree. They never switched with each other—ever. They were all just being who they always were, behaving as the person they were yesterday and were again today. They were all just doing what they do.

George was a great guy, but I knew at eight years old that Georgie Porgie couldn't change by his own free will, or else he would have. I realized that we would all change things about ourselves if it was simply a matter of mustering up the desire to do so. Georgie Porgie genuinely wanted to remember to bring the nail to school, but it still didn't happen. And my dad couldn't consciously will for himself the desire, or the ability, to see the world from a wider perspective, or he probably would have.

My profound spiritual awakening from the demonstration of the Pass the Jelly Principle could not be denied. The evidence of the principle was there all along. It was only a matter of seeing the obvious: *People do what they do. That's what they do. And* that *is it.*

Your What Hurts?

The staff at Dave's Auto Body said they'd call me in a few days after the insurance adjuster examined my car. I was now stranded, so I called my brother Bill to come pick me up, and I sat down to await his arrival.

Outside Dave's office doors were the accommodations located outside all automotive establishments: a well-weathered set of three plastic bucket seats. Orange, of course. I sat my individual right and left butt cheeks in the pre-formed indentations designed just for that purpose and relaxed into the swaddling comfort provided by the classic plastic mold. The chair was a perfect fit for the human form. The support I was receiving from such a simple design was remarkable. I couldn't help but speculate that this exact chair mold, made of recycled DVDs of *An Inconvenient Truth* could be sold for a handsome profit at trendy stores all across America. Some tag line like "comfort and global consciousness is always worth the price" would probably do the trick.

As the warm sun gave me a moment to bask in the glory of my own vitamin D production I noticed a young man shuffling toward me with a satchel of newspapers slung over his shoulder. He was a scruffy guy wearing a t-shirt with the rigid lettering that a heavy metal band would use for its logo. As he got closer I could make out the words *Serpentine Boards*. A surfing snake was below the lettering with what looked like a fellow surfer impaled by the snake's fangs. It instantly brought me back to all those Zen-like moments I used to enjoy out on the ocean battling for waves with all the stoned, angry surfers.

"Free *Union Tribune*?" he asked. "It's got knowledge, dude."

Dude is one of those dangerous universal words that are abused in San Diego. It's similar to *like* and *totally* that can easily become grammatical crack cocaine. They're addictive and can cause delusions. Habitual users often believe they are still conversant members of society, when it fact, they are not. I mean like totally, dude.

When I first arrived in San Diego the constant use of the word *dude* by those around me seemed odd, so I paid attention and became attuned to its diverse and nuanced usage. First, there's the lazy man's greeting, "Dude." Then there is the angry or aggressive scold, "Dude!" And the low-toned, slow-paced expression of depression, "Duuuude." The high-pitched expression of joy, excitement, or surprise, "Dude!" A polite, gently stated *pardon me*, "Dude." The astonished, *you are an idiot*, "Dude." Or my favorite, the answer to the inquisitive, "How's it going, dude?" being the apathetic, "Dude."

"I would love a newspaper," I said, holding out my hand. "Thank you."

"Would you like to sign up for a free, three-month subscription? You can cancel at any time."

"No, thank you. I go to Google News every day," I replied, my empty hand still extended.

"Oh."

There was a substantial pause, but we both sensed more words were coming. No one panicked, and I didn't interrupt, as that would be rude. We just had to be patient as his neurons mucked through the layers of THC in his brain.

"Do you mind if I give this paper to someone else then?" he asked.

"I think that would be great."

My charitable response gave him a visible sense of relief. I'm sure he didn't want to feel like one of those people who gives you something and then takes it back. What's the phrase for that? Oh never mind, I'm sure it's politically incorrect these days, so it's probably good that neither of us can think of it.

"No waves today, dude?" I inquired.

"No, dude. Benihana."

"Benihana?" I parroted back.

"Chop, chop, choppy, bro. Chop, chop, choppy," he said as he turned away.

The buoyant satisfaction of having blown my cover as an authentic dude made his satchel just a bit lighter as he bounced off into the distance. He sauntered past two bright red DO NOT ENTER: ENTRANCE ONLY signs. They were posted like sentries at the end of each wall that defined the sides of the parking lot entrance. He moseyed over the words, ONE WAY, painted on the asphalt with accompanying gigantic arrows pointing from the street up into the parking lot. I appreciated the directional enthusiasm of the building's owner. No one could accuse him of not being clear.

As my newspaper-coveting friend faded into the distance, I thought how much my brother Bill would have enjoyed meeting him. Like everybody else, Bill was going through life just doing what he does. Although in his case, doing what he does often turned out to be more entertaining than it is with other folks. He enjoyed nothing more than poking people in ways they didn't quite expect, just to see what happened. And believe me, things happened.

In the beginning, Bill's taunting techniques were those used by little brothers the world over. These methods were the standard skill set for getting back at older siblings who had wronged them in some way. But like all great artists, Bill had evolved his expertise to a place where people knew they were witnessing something special, even if they couldn't quite understand it. When his skills were on display, it was obvious to the most casual observer that he was worthy of the extra attention he so often received. Everybody is good at something, and Bill's special flare for human interaction was an area where he was a true master.

I spotted Bill's black Honda Civic at the traffic light. We caught each other's eyes and waved. I collected my belongings and began walking down the entryway to meet him. Bill turned up the entryway, coming directly toward me, when a white Ford Taurus zoomed past, going the wrong way, in an attempt to use the entrance as an exit.

The white Taurus raced past all the warning signs telling him *not* to do what he was doing. I couldn't help but appreciate the driver's willingness to defy common protocol. It is that spirit, after all, by which our human species progresses. I sensed that the driver was an optimist at heart. He was probably one of those people who go right to the very front of the shopping mall to find a parking space. Pessimists never get those spots up front because they never try. That's just the way it is.

The two cars met in the middle of the walled passageway. It was too narrow for either to pass. They bottlenecked. The front fender of each car stopped just before it reached the other's driver's side door. Neither car could go any further. They were at an impasse.

Once again, being a master of the obvious, I knew this was a situation where people were going to do exactly what they do. I mean really, how could they not? My brother looked directly at the other driver. His face displayed a stunning purity of indifference as he slowly threw up both this hands like the giant touchdown Jesus outside Notre Dame's football stadium. To the casual observer my brother's actions simply said, "I've got the right of way, dude. You're going to have to back up," but to those looking deeper, it meant much more.

It appeared as though the driver of the other vehicle was either an employee of the auto body shop or was at least very familiar with the parking lot. I could see that a shortcut out the entryway could save him from having to go all the way around the block to get on the freeway, but none of that mattered now. I was about to witness another mesmerizing display of human interaction.

The two drivers locked eyes and I do believe the forces at play for the gentleman in the Ford Taurus were simply more than he could bear. The tattoos up his arms, the girlfriend in the passenger seat, and a fair quantity of paint fumes inhaled all morning were a volatile mix. In the end, brother Bill's nonchalance could only be interpreted as a blatant display of hostility.

"You got a fucking problem?" Tatty Man politely asked with his head tilted out the window.

Brother Bill's response to Tatty Man's inquiry was not the standard fare that most of us were used to. Bill served a custom recipe for his new friend, using only the freshest ingredients. He plated a loud, rapid-fire, mumble of words, said in a way that caused intense visceral annoyance. For added pleasure, Bill accompanied his words with a facial expression somewhat like a white guy, which my brother is, trying to imitate a Chinese shopkeeper.

"Your-what-hurts?" Bill offered.

Tatty Man scrunched his face in a look of disbelief and shock. He seemed genuinely confused by brother Bill's response, so in the interest of clarity, he tried again.

"I said, you got a fucking problem?"

"Your-what-hurts?" the only reply.

The slightly more enthusiastic, yet no less annoying reply from Bill made the girlfriend in Tatty Man's car begin to giggle, which absolutely infuriated her man.

"What the fuck did you say?" Tatty Man erupted.

As only a pro could, Bill decided to mix things up a bit. First, he jabbed Tatty Man with his finest British butler accent.

"I said, good sir…"

Then in the unbelievably annoying, rapid-fire speech (with facial expression added at no extra charge), he delivered his signature blow.

"Your-what-hurts?"

The girlfriend in the other car could contain herself no longer. She burst into full-blown laughter while slapping the dashboard with one hand and holding her stomach with the other. I'm convinced that Tatty Man still had no idea what my brother was saying. He was about to have an aneurism from a deadly mixture of utter confusion and absolute frustration, a cocktail Bill had mixed just for him.

"Why, you motherfucker. That's it," Tatty Man shot back.

He stepped out of the car to reveal a body that had many large muscles underneath his many large tattoos. His white, wife-beater t-shirt added just the right touch to make it look as though my brother had made a big mistake. Tatty Man stood in front of Bill's car flexing his muscles, squeezing his fists, and sizing up the guy he was planning on pile-driving into the ground.

Brother Bill, being much smaller and weaker, decided it would be a grand time to jump out of his car and begin doing a most excellent imitation of the Cowardly Lion from *The Wizard of Oz*. He closed his fists and held them up in front of his face like an old-time fighter as his legs moved back and forth like an Irish clog dancer.

"Put 'em up. Put 'em up, I say," he said in a dopey Lion voice. "Put 'em up. I'll fight you with one hand tied behind my back. I'll fight you standing on one leg. Put 'em up."

The Cowardly Lion imitation put the girlfriend of Tatty Man over the top. Her cries of laughter howled out the car toward her now beyond-enraged boyfriend. He had taken enough abuse, and he was going to make my brother pay. I must admit that I was a bit concerned. I should have guessed that my brother would know just what button to push next. After all, it is what he does.

Tatty Man's latex-tight t-shirt was complemented by a pair of low-slung jeans with red boxers covering the top of his otherwise exposed butt. His work boots were the short man's equivalent of pumps. They had an extra inch of heel added for the illusion of height. These lower body fashion decisions inhibited his ability to move in the agile manner that would be required to catch my brother. When Tatty began climbing over the hoods of the conjoined cars, Bill jumped over the three-foot-high cement barrier beside him in one graceful motion.

Tatty took a bit of time to awkwardly negotiate the barrier with his crotch-at-the-kneecaps pants. Brother Bill used the delay to demonstrate a mocking interest in Tatty's barrier climb with a hand placed under his nodding chin. He did this because he was a true professional and didn't want the audience getting bored while we waited for the next scene to manifest.

Once Tatty was ready, the activities resumed with Bill running away from him in a physical style reminiscent of Herman Munster fleeing from a mouse. Manic sounds of glee and terror accompanied his spastic running style as he expertly kept the pace at just the right intensity to remain enticing to his pursuer.

Tatty's stride was only two feet long, and he had to pull his pants back up every fourth step. Brother Bill, on the other hand, was an All-American, sub-four-minute miler in college. His repeated stunning bursts of speed right before capture were the giveaway. The handicappers in Vegas picked right up on this and set the odds of Tatty catching my brother at somewhere around 753 to 1.

"Come on, baby, you can git 'em," Tatty's girlfriend laughed as she cheered on her man. "That's it. You wear him down baby. You git 'em baby. That's right."

It was clear that the level of frustration Tatty Man was experiencing must have been unfathomable. When I added up all the elements, I was pretty sure I'd never seen a greater exercise in human futility. And yet all of this was just a wonderful display of people doing what they do. The scene being played out had it all: right of way vs. do not enter, weak vs. strong, fast vs. slow, annoying vs. angry, function vs. fashion. There was even a damsel in distress to go along with the court jester.

It was an impressive display of mastership by both my brother and Tatty Man. I was honored to be in their presence. My brother's mastery was obvious, but I was also impressed with Tatty Man's total lack of resistance to his uncontrollable rage. Tatty's resulting mindbending irritation was something most people would be simply unwilling to subject themselves to. I was in the presence of true greatness wherever I looked.

Tatty Man was completely winded after three minutes of what began to resemble some strange mating ritual. Bill had skillfully led him to the far end of the parking lot and left him hunched over with both hands on his knees. He couldn't take another step. With his work complete, Bill glided back over to his car.

"All set?" he asked, like he had just returned from the men's room at the Exxon station.

We got in the car and both gave the girlfriend a warm wave good-bye. She returned a friendly wave with her right hand and covered a guilty giggle with her left.

"I like her," Bill announced, like he had just met Tatty's girlfriend at a weekend barbecue.

"Me, too, Bill," I said. "Me, too."

We backed out of the entrance, and a mile or so down the road there was a minor traffic jam. As we approached, I spotted Not Jim hooking the carcass of a car to the back of his truck. Brother Bill and I were caught in the lane of traffic that was blocked. A gap appeared in front of a silver minivan to our left, and my brother began to pull out. Upon seeing this, the driver of the minivan laid on the gas to make sure we could not squeeze into *her* lane.

Bill's window was still rolled down from his driver's education exercise with Tatty Man. For reasons known only to the gods, the driver of the silver minivan also had her passenger side window rolled down. Bill's entry had been blocked, but the minivan was also blocked from moving forward by the car in front of it. The driver of the minivan, being exactly who she is at all times, just couldn't resist looking over at the person whose attempt at merging she had single-handedly thwarted. Beaming with self-worth, she looked over at brother Bill.

With no prior planning or thought on his part, Bill stuck his entire head out his driver's side window. Then with a freakishly rubberized neck and a head bouncing back and forth like a bobble-head doll, he looked at the woman driver and let out the most confusing sound my brain has ever tried to unravel.

Imagine an overexcited, harmless but hyperactive patient in a psych ward. Now imagine the sound he would make when he found out they were serving his favorite fish sticks for lunch in the cafeteria. Now ramp it up so that it's at about one hundred decibels. Oddly, that will get you most of the way there. There was literally no place in her brain, or mine, to put such a sound.

The poor woman driver. Only seconds earlier she was fully enamored with her own personal power and flaunting it shamelessly. Now she was fully brain-cramped. Brother Bill's shocking display of mental instability had caused all the gears in her brain to lock.

You've probably heard of the fight-or-flight response that our bodies will produce when we feel threatened. Well, Bill had apparently accessed the little-known *confusion* response. The woman driving the minivan sat frozen in absolute awe. I think Bill may have actually been providing a type of religious experience for her, perhaps a rebirth of some kind, but we'll never know. The traffic started moving, and the car behind her leaned on its horn.

Fortunately, the driver behind our friend in the minivan waved us in and Bill pulled into the gap in traffic. The silver minivan was now directly in front of us. We had the perfect view of the purple bumper sticker that had been applied to her right rear bumper. The white lettering on it read: "Practice Random Kindness and Senseless Acts of Beauty." Bill and I both read the bumper sticker at the same time.

"That, my brotha'…" he said in the high-pitched voice of a black Southern Baptist preacher, "is sweeeeeeeeeeeeeet."

"Yes it is, my brother," I said. "Yes, it is."

The *way* of brother Bill had led to an awe-inspiring ride home. I couldn't help but wonder how he had remained completely unscathed over the years. With the antics he pulls on a regular basis, it's amazing that no real harm has come to him. Maybe it's because he never *really* hurts anyone; he just instinctively reaches inside their psyche and effortlessly twists it in any way he chooses.

He's like an odd type of superhero. I would call him Mirror Man. He's a normal everyday man to most people, but if you're lucky, he'll assist you in experiencing all those things about yourself that are hidden just below the surface. If you poke at Bill just right, he's suddenly wearing a cape and holding a mirror in front of you. You think it's him, but it never is—it's you. It's always you, with all your own stuff, and he's just there to point it out for all to see.

Brother Bill would be the first to tell you that he has no idea how or why he does what he does. It's just what he does. It's a true talent, a gift really, but if you think about it, I guess we're all gifted in our own way.

Should Have

Bill and I drove down the freeway and passed a series of billboards depicting the wonders to be found at the famous San Diego Zoo. I recalled how visiting the Slater Park Zoo in Pawtucket, Rhode Island, was one of my family's regular activities when I was a child. It was free, and it was close. Every few weeks we'd pile five kids and two parents into our metallic green Ford Grand Torino station wagon and off we'd go. The parents sat up front, the three sisters were stationed in the middle seat, and my little brother and I were assigned to the "jump seat" in the very back.

Since air conditioning was obviously only for rich people, we went with the less effective open-all-the-windows-to-be-cooled-by-hot-air method. It's kind of like trying to cool off with a blow drier set on hot. The method included opening the car's very back window, which allowed for maximum carbon monoxide inhalation by my brother and me.

Ford had obviously done extensive research on the precise shape and location of the car's tail pipe. It must have delivered the perfect dosage of exhaust because I never heard of any children dying. Between the sedative effects of the fumes and trying to go unnoticed as we tossed items out the back window, the jump seat made for a very pleasant journey. My dad probably noticed how "calm" we were when he opened the rear window for us, so he always made sure it was rolled all the way down.

These were also the days when you would stick your head out the window as the gas station attendant (yes, like the buffalo, they were once seen all across America) was filling the gas tank. This way you could fully realize the joy of smelling gasoline fumes.

"I love the smell of gasoline," I would tell my mom between inhalations.

"Whatever makes you happy, dear," was her motto.

I'm pretty sure that today I'd be shoved into therapy for fear I'd become a huffer—you know, one of those people who inhales gasoline fumes for the high it gives them. Of course, therapy was unnecessary. I remained a mere social huffer, a casual huffer at best. I never bought the gasoline myself. Yet, to this day, with no gas station attendant in sight, I do find myself "not avoiding" the gasoline fumes as I fill up my tank. Ahhh, the sweet smell of gasoline, the memories of partial carbon monoxide poisoning while sitting seatbelt-free in the back of an open-windowed station wagon. Good times, good times.

The jump seat in the Grand Torino was beyond the reach of my parents and facing the opposite direction from all the other passengers. It's as close to a chauffeur-driven limousine as I've gotten to this very day. I found the sensation of facing backwards in a moving car to be quite pleasing. It was much more exciting to notice where you had just been than to be bored by something you'd been looking at the entire time you approached it.

Maybe I found it so stimulating because it was a more realistic way of experiencing things. In life, we're actually only experiencing what has just happened. We don't really get to see what's coming up, no matter how much we like to pretend that we can.

After twenty-five minutes in the jump seat, my brother and I would arrive at the zoo primed and ready to go. We would very calmly get out of the back seat of the car as all young boys do when they arrive at a destination they have been eagerly anticipating. The entire family would then head into the zoo. Sometimes we'd hook up with one of the free zoo tours. Other times my dad and mom would just set us free to roam unsupervised among all the other animals.

My brother and I had no money to purchase proper food to feed the animals, nor did we bring any stale Wonder Bread as did many other families. It was widely understood at the time that all animals love Wonder Bread. It must be the fortified, enriched, bleached, white flour. I guess animals really do have a natural instinct about what's good for them.

My brother and I were left to scrounge from whatever others had left behind. As much as it horrifies me today, I'm still amazed at what a billy goat can eat. We would feed them plastic bags that carrots or apples came in. They would eat cigarette butts and candy wrappers. The same goats were there every time we would visit the zoo, apparently no worse off for the nonfood items they had ingested, but I still cringe a bit when I think about it today.

Our all-time favorite activity was feeding the giraffes. They were kept in an area with a cement walkway that was always covered in shallow puddles of muddy water. Somewhere along the way, my brother and I figured out an entertaining game. The goal was to find a piece of Wonder Bread that some little kid had dropped in one of the puddles, yet which was still white on one side. If you fed that piece of bread to the giraffe with the white side facing up, the giraffe would take it in its mouth until it realized that it was a disgusting, dirt-soaked, imitation of a piece of bread. The giraffe would then spit it out from his 12-foot-high position and spew it over the entire crowd.

Naturally, my brother and I would be out of range by the time the spitting began, but it was still very dramatic for everyone in the audience. They seemed genuinely excited about such an authentic interaction with nature. We felt it was the least we could do as regular visitors to the zoo. It was just our little way of giving back.

One day, my father witnessed my brother and me doing our giraffe trick. He was mortified when, by the third iteration, he realized we were doing it on purpose. For some reason feeding goats plastic bags was not a punishable offense, but the spewing-giraffe trick crossed some imaginary line in my father's mind. Maybe it was the screaming spectators? We'll probably never know. My father gave us a quick, paternity-denying, come-here-now wave of his right hand. We hesitated, but then he clenched his teeth, so we knew we were busted.

"Get over here," he snapped in a voice that was intense but that wouldn't draw the attention of the other zoo visitors.

My brother and I walked over to him slowly, giving him a little time to cool.

"What are you two doing?" he demanded.

"We're feeding the giraffes," I answered innocently.

"You're feeding them dirty bread that they're going to spit on people," he corrected.

He waited for a reply, but my brother and I employed the brilliant strategy of remaining silent. My father knew that the longer he stood with us, the more people would figure out he was the individual who had spawned us, so he caved pretty quickly.

"Let's go find your mother," he grumbled.

We met up with the rest of the family at the polar bear cages. To the untrained eye, the cages themselves seemed quite idiot-proof. A six-foot-wide, four-foot-deep moat separated the human beings from the actual cage. The moat was usually full of water, but on this day it was dry. Even without the water, the distance and barriers preventing contact with the bear seemed an acceptable deterrent. However, for one woman the dry moat was a glaring gap in security that she was simply incapable of resisting.

We've all been in situations where we feel we're the exception to the rules, so I can understand her frustration. She may have been an experienced *National Geographic* photographer or a guest host on one of the *Wild Kingdom* episodes I had missed. Maybe she had multiple degrees in zoology or done extensive work with polar bears in the Alaskan wilderness. Whatever the reason, what this lady was about to do must have made perfect sense in her own mind.

The pleasantly plump (almost like a little seal), thirty-ish woman, with the full support and encouragement of her husband, climbed over the three-foot-high fence, scooted on her butt down the inclined side of the moat, walked across the dry moat, and yes, leaned against the metal crossbar on top of the far cement wall that was just a few feet from the bars of the cage.

At first, the bear seemed not to notice her because someone on the opposite side of the cage was tossing him Wonder Bread, but she had a solution for that.

"Here, Mr. Bear. Here, Mr. Bear," she yelled.

Her commitment to getting a good photo did not go unnoticed by Mr. Bear. With much enthusiasm, he dove into the pool and began swimming toward the woman who was waving a big piece of meat at him, better known as an "arm."

When Mr. Bear arrived at the woman's desired location, she turned her back to the bear so that her husband could get some realistic photographs. Mr. Bear was doing his very best to get a hold of his awareness-challenged prey, but his paws were wider than the spaces in the bar, so it was taking him some time to figure things out. The woman continued laughing and smiling while her husband clicked away with his camera. The action photos of his wife and the bear were certainly going to be a big hit at the next family gathering.

The laughing subsided when Mr. Bear got his arm through the bars in a way that he could pin the woman's shoulder against the crossbar that ran along the top of the wall. It seemed to come as a surprise that the thousand-pound polar bear was much stronger than she was. Freeing herself was proving to be difficult. As she struggled, she seemed more annoyed that the bear was ruining her picture than she was afraid that she might be eaten. Fortunately, the bear was unable to do much more than hold her in place.

As you may have guessed, adults began screaming and running for the zoo staff. Moms and kids were immediately bursting with projectile tears. Oddly, the woman being attacked was relatively calm and seemed to be approaching her predicament like she was trying to change a flat tire on her car. She knew that the polar bear attached to her shoulder was a bit of a problem, but nothing that couldn't be dealt with once she acquired the proper tools. She and the bear seemed to be at a stalemate.

At this point, her husband had the shocking realization that his wife's situation might be less than perfectly safe. He decided to rescue his damsel in distress, and in one smooth move caught his left foot on the top of the barrier and fell head first onto the cement below. He saved the camera from being harmed, but looked like he would need a few stitches in his forehead.

As the husband collected himself, the zoo staff came on the scene like a fairly well organized SWAT team. They quickly persuaded the bear that a bucket of some really stinky food was better than the woman's arm he had been dreaming of consuming. The fact that the woman had doubled-down on stupid didn't seem to play into the bear's decision.

The woman was basically unharmed, and I noticed no lobotomy scars on her temples as the zoo staff escorted her into an ambulance with her injured husband. My brother and I agreed that the husband would probably need a tetanus shot because we always got one when we went to the emergency room. We also couldn't wait to go to school on Monday and tell everyone about the coolest thing we'd ever seen.

I was also slightly pleased that I had learned a valuable lesson about polar bears that might come in handy when I'm the co-host of *Wild Kingdom*: a stinky bucket of food can save a life. I also learned that when it comes to Mother Nature, love her, respect her, but never—and I do mean never—turn your back on her. This is especially true if you are being viewed as part of the food chain.

"I hope you kids know to never do that," my dad said during the car ride home.

It was the standard, obligatory, 20/20 hindsight, parental statement. It was said in the same tone as when my dad unknowingly took us to the movie *The Bad News Bears*, where the foul-mouthed child, Tanner, used every curse word in the book.

"I hope you kids never use language like that," was his comment after the movie.

It's interesting that the same boilerplate warning from Dad after these two events yielded completely different outcomes. I was quite sure I would never climb across a barrier to get up close and personal with one of nature's greatest predators (I still haven't to this day). However, using foul language was quite in vogue at Newman Elementary School. I was never a slave to the latest trend, but this one had a strange appeal. It seemed relatively harmless to quote some of Tanner's prime lines from the movie, so I swore like everyone else when no adults were around.

As we drove home I once again inhaled enough carbon monoxide so that the world began to take on a certain mystical quality. The zoo tended to wear us kids out, so everyone in the car was rather calm. My brother and I sat backwards in the jump seat tossing pebbles out the back window, and my sisters sat sweating as they argued about who had touched who first.

"What was she thinking? Unbelievable," my father blurted out.

We all knew he was referring to the polar bear woman. The others in the car demonstrated their agreement, as would any good serf in the feudal system that was our family, with silent nods of affirmation. However, I sensed that the word *unbelievable* had been purposely dropped as a clue.

Like any true master, my father was not straight-out asking a question, but rather testing my understanding of deeper principles. He never actually said this. I could just tell. The others in the car never caught on to the deeper game being played, but since the recent demonstration of the Pass the Jelly Principle, I had learned to pay much closer attention. I took a nice deep breath, and a quote I had copied down months earlier in my Dr. Seuss Notebook, Quotebook, Look-What-I-Wrote Book came crashing down upon me like a Zen master's staff. Maybe it was more like a hockey stick, but you get the idea.

"Minds are like rivers—they eventually flow where they must," I said without really thinking about it.

The quote momentarily stunned all passengers in the car, but they quickly shook it off and seemed no worse for the wear. My father then posed another life-changing question.

"Why would she think she could get away with that?"

The fact that I had awakened to the Pass the Jelly Principle earlier that year did make the entire polar bear incident less shocking for me than for the others. Frankly, "people doing what they do" had become more fascinating and less confusing with each passing day. My father's demonstration reaped continuing benefits.

It was so obvious once you saw it. People everywhere have thoughts and feelings that rise up in their minds. Some thoughts and feelings are ignored and others are acted upon, but the thoughts and feelings (or lack thereof) are what steer us. The woman who had just tried to feed herself to a polar bear had some thought like, "I'd just love to get a close-up photo with that big white bear." As far as thoughts go, I'm sure it was a common one for people standing at a polar bear cage.

The woman also had thoughts like, "That bear is cute, and white, and fluffy. He's got a name. He's around people all the time. I'm sure he's one of those tame polar bears. It would be safe to stand right next to him and have my husband snap a few photos." And while those thoughts are a bit more unusual, I'm sure they aren't entirely uncommon.

What truly made the situation rare was that her husband had a similar perception of the situation *and* they were two people who were willing to blatantly disregard rules. Only when you mix all those elements together does it become attack time at the zoo.

It's also possible that Darwin was right and these people were just finding a situation where they could be weeded out of the population. As much as we might like it to be so, there really are no lifeguards at the gene pool. Either way, they weren't consciously controlling the way they perceived the situation. As wrong as their perception was, they weren't consciously trying to harm themselves.

They simply weren't aware that their perception was only a perception and not reality.

As I sat on my knees, facing the backs of the rest of my family, I felt the warm breeze of my father's faith in me. He knew I had to figure this out for myself or the lesson wouldn't stick. I looked around at the other six people in the car and realized that each person was continuously having their own completely unique experience. We all have our own unique perceptions, our own unique thoughts, and our own unique feelings as we meet life, and we really don't control what these are. It all just kind of pops into our heads. We may assume we're experiencing the exact same reality as others when we move through the world, yet nothing could be further from the truth.

"She should have known not to do such a stupid thing," the master behind the steering wheel added.

The thoroughness of my father's teaching did not go unnoticed. He was now mixing in a little Socratic dialogue to drive the point home. His range was impressive.

"But she didn't," I said.

"But she should have," my father replied, with a substantial increase in volume on the word *should*.

Feeling relatively safe in the jump seat of the car, I was comfortable with pushing the master a little further than usual.

"But she *didn't* know."

At this point, I caught my father's eyes in the rearview mirror as he glared back at me. With a firmness that I could truly appreciate, even from the very back seat of the car, he reiterated his teaching.

"But she *should* have."

For reasons still unknown, but probably stress-related, I thought my father might appreciate an operatic response. My prepubescent, castrato voice lacked the power I was looking for, so I skipped right over tenor and went straight for baritone. In the deepest voice I could muster, I rocked from side to side and pounded on the imaginary big, brass kettledrum in front of me.

"Buuut sheee diiid nnn't," I sang as I slapped the top of the seat with each syllable.

My father glared at me and then glanced over at my mother. I could see the thought rise up in his mind, "At best, paternity is questionable." His mind went back to my mother's whereabouts nine months before I was born, but then he realized I had his eyes, so he tried again.

"But she *should* have."

"She either did or she didn't," I said, "If she knew better, she wouldn't have done it. But she didn't know better, so she did it. I don't understand *should. "*

"Because, she should have. Unbelievable," my dad said, taking both hands off the steering wheel and hurling them skyward in frustration.

I knew this was another important moment in my dad's teaching. He kept repeating the same words, which meant the rest of the lesson was up to me to figure out. Plus, there was a chance he would pull over and stop the car. Then the lesson would take an entirely different turn. I spun around and sat down in the jump seat, took a nice deep breath of carbon monoxide, and contemplated the teaching that had just taken place.

The conversation had caused a very loud silence amongst the other passengers. I, however, was in the zone. I was picking up all of my father's subtle clues, somewhat effortlessly I might add. Though not perceptible to anyone else in the vehicle, the word *unbelievable* that he added to the end of his last statement seemed to be a deliberate message. I surmised he must be letting me know that my detailed understanding was wonderful, but I should not be distracted by it. It still all came back to the original Pass the Jelly Principle: people are always doing what they do. This was true regardless of what deeper insights might be realized.

At the very moment I was contemplating the life-altering implications of this spiritual lesson, my sisters were all poking at each other and pretty much oblivious to anything else. My mother was most likely praying for my physical well-being. My father had begun humming some old person's tune, and my brother was busy throwing pebbles out the back window.

I relaxed back into my seat and took a nice deep breath, whether or not I *should*. As I came to a new point of equilibrium with the fumes, another profound understanding arose into my consciousness. I thought about the people in this hot, gas-guzzling, metallic green beast of an automobile and how they all were just doing what they do. Me, them, and everyone else on the planet, were just doing what they do. It's a natural human tendency to "should" on people, but there is only the actuality of what happens in life. The rest is just a story, no matter who's telling it.

It seems life's most important lessons are often given free of charge. This lesson was no exception.

Raw Boy

After an event-filled ride from Dave's Auto Body, brother Bill dropped me off safely at home. I was unable to attach a warning label to him before he pulled away, so I could only speculate as to what might happen on his way back to work. With no car at my disposal, I hopped on my bike and pedaled down the street to Henry's Health Food Store. After abiding by the words of the ancient masters, "Trust the Universe, but lock your bicycle," I headed into the store.

I passed through the automatic doors and took a free sample of some delicious Russian kefir. I sipped the tiny cup of drinkable yogurt and surveyed the grazing shoppers. I'd stumbled across many lessons in habitats such as these over the years, so I was always on the lookout for new teachers. The nourishing of our bodies is a basic human need, and as a member of the species, I find the various approaches people take in this endeavor to be forever fascinating.

The first lesson I ever learned in a health food store was to be very careful around vegans. For those of you not in the know, a vegan adheres to the strictest of vegetarian diets. Technically, fruitarians and breatharians are stricter, but they don't usually live long enough to acquire any substantial populations. Basically, back in the 1940s, the vegans removed the "etari" from the word veg*etari*an to come up with the word *vegan*. Like the new word, a vegan diet has even less in it than a standard vegetarian one. Whereas vegetarians won't eat animals, a vegan won't eat animals or animal products of any kind. Vegans shun the eggs and dairy products that many vegetarians rely on as a vital source of protein.

But please, be careful. Vegans may appear to be the ultimate pacifists on the outside, but they're a feisty lot. They all agree that dairy products are not allowed, but after that it gets a bit fuzzy. Stay away from the topic of honey if you can, unless you have a fair bit of time on your hands. Yes, I'm referring to honey from honeybees. It's a gray area in the vegan community, and you might be in for a long dissertation. Some think it's an animal product, and some don't. The bees have apparently been vague about whether they're doing production or manufacturing. Honestly, I've yet to pick a side myself.

Oh, and don't even think of mentioning silk. The fabric is made using silkworms and vegans can get very upset about the entire enterprise. The exploitation of billions, perhaps trillions of worms over the centuries is not to be taken lightly. Heads have literally rolled over this topic. Sure, they were heads of lettuce, but they still rolled, and it wasn't pretty. As a matter of fact, I'd steer clear of all cloth-related topics, or you may find yourself limited to wearing only organic jute finery, which is known to chafe.

Another lesson I learned through painful repetition was that the phrase *vegan dessert* is self-canceling. There are many delicious vegan dishes in the world, and there are many tasty desserts in the world, but I've yet to find a delicious vegan dessert. It's due solely to their lack of dairy products. Others disagree, but then I see the red stain on their upper lip from drinking the vegan Kool-Aid, so I just smile. Any non-Kool-Aid-drinking doubters are welcome to go to your local health food store and sample a vegan brownie; I suspect you will quickly realize the wisdom in my words.

I had wandered over to the supplement section of the store and began perusing the shelves for the product I was seeking. For any disorder you can think of, there is a supplement of some kind that promises to do the trick. Since words such as "natural," "clinical studies," and many others on the labels don't actually mean what the average person thinks they mean, finding an effective supplement is a bit of a crapshoot.

As in much of life, you can't assume we are all talking about the same thing just because we're using the same words. When this is done unintentionally, it's called miscommunication. When it's done intentionally, it's called marketing. I've found marketing people to be some of the greatest teachers of life lessons. It is because of them that I've learned to ask two important questions: *What do you mean?* and *How do you know?* It's amazing how quickly these two questions can clarify a conversation.

Still, the problem lies in knowing which supplements really work and which ones don't. I often feel like a miner seeing shiny specks of gold in the river below, but not knowing if it's fool's gold until I can get my hands on it and test it myself. That's where the marketing people come into play. How else is one to learn anything in life if you can't make some mistakes along the way and purchase a few claims full of shiny, well-marketed pyrite? Marketing teams throughout the world allow us to learn through experience.

"Make sure to soak your nuts overnight. It makes a big difference," I heard an employee recommend to the male customer he was assisting.

I realized long ago that context is everything in our conversations with others, so I took a moment to notice the almonds in the man's shopping cart. After a sigh of relief for the gentleman, I realized he was probably trying out a raw food diet and was getting advice from a professional. Through way too much time spent in health food stores, I've also observed that the raw-food-only types tend to be ultra thin and have a rather manic energy about them. The employee fit the bill, so when the man and his nuts walked away, I took a guess.

"Are you a raw foodist?" I asked the worker in the supplement section.

"Yes, I am. How did you know?" Raw Boy replied.

"Oh, you just have that look about you."

"Well, thank you."

"You're very welcome."

"Can I help you with anything?" Raw Boy asked.

"Yes, I was wondering what you think of zinc supplements. I just read an article that said up to 75 percent of adult males have a zinc deficiency. Do you know if that's true?"

"That sounds about right."

A knowing nod of his head added the certitude I was seeking. I'd looked at all the unbiased "clinical studies" provided free of charge by the supplement industry and concluded that my body was screaming for some zinc. The literature had also convinced me that my prostate was right on the verge of falling out of my body, so the question that followed was predictable.

"Is it true that zinc is important for prostate health?"

"It's true. It says so on most of the labels. I've been taking zinc daily, since I was thirty-three." Raw Boy professed.

"Wow," I said, thinking this guy was in his early fifties but looked like he was about forty-five. "How old are you?"

"I'm thirty-eight, my friend."

"That's amazing. I'm in. I'll go with the large bottle."

I was going to buy the zinc regardless of virtually any information I received at the store. It's what I went there to do. Like most people,

I was just seeking advice that would confirm a decision I'd already made. It's similar to the Blue Blocker sunglasses I purchased from an infomercial. I resisted for months, but all my efforts were a futile attempt to avoid the inevitable. For some reason the purchasing center of my brain was flipped on by the commercial the first time I saw it. When they offered the two-for-one deal, I immediately dialed the eight hundred number before I could change my mind, just so I could get on with my life.

Raw Boy turned and began organizing the shelf across from me, but I had one small question left.

"Can I just take a capsule before my morning coffee?" I asked, not knowing the raw, organic, nongenetically engineered wrath that was about to rain down upon me.

His head spun violently toward me and his eyeballs became four sizes too big instead of just two.

"Coffee is the downfall of Western civilization, second only to alcohol," he said emphatically.

Ahhh, the sweet aroma of people doing what they do was brewing right in front of me. I just knew I was going to like Raw Boy the moment I saw him.

"What do you mean?" I asked.

"What do I mean?" he repeated. "Just look around at all these people running around all hyped up on coffee."

"How do you know that's the cause of our freneticism? There could be many reasons behind these changes in our culture," I said.

"I know because every year coffee consumption increases, and every year our culture gets worse."

"By that reasoning, couldn't people's increased consumption of health supplements every year be the cause?"

"Vitamins and supplements are good for you. Coffee is not," Raw Boy replied.

"Coffee makes me a better person," I said in a friendly tone. "It increases blood flow to my brain, which makes me feel good. That's why everyone drinks it. It makes us happier and more productive."

"What are you talking about?" Raw Boy exclaimed. "Are you an apologist for the multinational coffee conglomerate that exploits millions of migrant workers daily throughout the world?"

"No, I drink Fair Trade coffee. I find the slave flavor of regular coffee bothers my intestines."

"Well, that still doesn't take away from the fact that coffee is ruining Western culture."

I'm generally a live-and-let-live kind of guy, but Raw Boy was insulting my muse, and I just couldn't allow it. I rushed to her aid with a brief history lesson.

"You may want to consider that coffee might actually be the *cause* of Western civilization, not its downfall."

"What do *you* mean?" Raw Boy challenged. "And how do *you* know?"

I was pleased that he was catching on to the game of "What do you mean? How do you know?" It's so much more fun when both sides play.

"I mean that in the sixteen hundreds, the average European drank three liters of beer a day. Everybody was drunk all day. It wasn't until coffee and tea were introduced into European culture that the entire population could synchronize first thing in the morning and we could actually *have* a Western culture. Coffee and black caffeinated tea were actually the lights that brought us out of the Dark Ages."

"How do you know that's true?" Raw Boy asked.

"I've read about these things in various sources, but ultimately, I don't know."

"Let me ask you a question," Raw Boy interjected. "If you don't drink coffee for a day or two, do you get a headache?"

"Absolutely."

"Well then, you're addicted. You're an addict."

I was impressed. His commitment to saving me (and being right) was filled with a passion that I found refreshing. I suppose Raw Boy thought I would be shamed into realizing the error of my ways. Perhaps he hoped I would repent on my knees before him and accept the supplement industry as my lord and savior. However, my love affair with coffee had begun long ago. After such an enduring and truly pleasurable relationship, I couldn't just let her go on a whim. My response to being outed as an addict was both heretical and unrepentant.

"Oh, I'm completely addicted. I'm a self-confessed Javacrucian. Every morning when I take my first sip of coffee, I say out loud, 'God, that's good.' "

"Coffee is the most anti-spiritual drink on the planet," he challenged.

I was pleased to see that his vast enthusiasm was not dampened by my light-hearted humor. After all, he had a right to his own opinion, just not his own facts.

"I suppose different viewpoints on topics makes the day more interesting for all of us," I said, smiling. "You might find it interesting that it was a Sufi monk who brewed the very first cup of coffee twelve hundred years ago. He loved it because it allowed him to stay up all night meditating."

"Really?"

"And it was another Sufi monk who risked his life to smuggle green coffee beans out of Yemen to his brother monks in India," I said. "He planted them at his monastery, high in the Indian mountains, where they spawned the rest of the coffee plants that exist all over the world today. So maybe coffee is actually the *most* spiritual drink on the planet. I've never heard of a monk risking his life for tea."

Just as I was finishing my riveting oral history of coffee a hummingbird of a woman in workout tights approached at hyperactive speed. She landed at my side, tilted her head back, and gulped what appeared to be the final remnants of a twenty-four-ounce barrel of coffee in her tiny hand. She waited a generous seven seconds for Raw Boy's assistance before speed dialing her friend and announcing to everyone in the vicinity that she was just standing around waiting to be served. Fortunately, her caffeine-induced A.D.D., which was apparently her substitute for manners, drew her attention elsewhere, and she buzzed over to a display at the far end of the isle. When she walked away, Raw Boy gave me a wide-eyed nod, indicating that the woman had just summarized his entire argument.

I laughed. Without a word, life had countered my unbridled support for coffee with an undeniable real life experience. The shock forced me to recall an image of my old meditation teacher saying, "Wisdom, in Buddhism, is defined as the proper and efficacious use of caffeine." I realized that the truth was probably somewhere in the middle of where Raw Boy and I had staked our positions. The answer appeared to be found on the most difficult path of all, the one of moderation.

"Oh, and coffee is really high in anti-oxidants, too," I added in the silence that followed, but even I could hear a slight echo as I spoke my hollow words.

Raw Boy and I were now stuck in neutral. We both knew that reality had just trumped any further arguments I would offer for unbounded coffee consumption, but there were also lines of well-mannered people at coffee shops all over America. Coffee was also not the plague upon Western civilization that Raw Boy claimed.

I could have taken this as a signal to leave; I mean, sometimes that's just the way it goes, but it seemed a shame. I knew there was a place where a new connection could be made, a place where our disagreements could fade into the background. I thought dropping a poetic Rumi bomb might do the trick. Something like, "Out beyond ideas of wrongdoing and rightdoing, there is a field. I'll meet you there…" but after a few hundredths of a second, I realized that would be a bad idea.

A quote like that exchanged between two unfamiliar males without some power tools in hand or a football game on the TV might be misinterpreted. He'd probably think I was trying to pick him up, and I didn't want that. Don't get me wrong; I have no problem with gay folks— my dick just doesn't point that way. The last thing I wanted to do was add sexual confusion to the situation. I'd end up walking out of the store with a useless, six-month supply of herbal Viagra.

I was stuck in a conversation that had obviously died, and nothing I was doing seemed to be working. It's in situations such as these that I've found the solution often lies in the direction opposite from where you would rationally think it would be. For instance, if your conversation with the Dalai Lama was waning, you could ask him something about *The Three Stooges*, since he's a fan. It's not a place most people would think to go, but if you knew to ask, you'd find yourself quickly right back on track.

I realized I had mistakenly tried to inject a taboo subject into my conversation with Raw Boy. He was thoroughly enjoying living the life of a health food store guru and didn't need my challenging views on the wonders of coffee. This store was his place of dominance. Every time someone would ask him a question, a little dopamine would spurt into his brain, and he'd get a buzz as he gave his answer.

It's not much different from smoking a cigarette, except for that whole lung cancer thing. We all get our little dopamine hits in life from the things that we're into. It could be Jesus, Buddha, politics, or colonics (those will really clear your head, by the way). I was being a dopamine buzz killer, which was not my intention. Then the saying came to mind, "There are no coincidences," which I think is total bullshit, so I figured that mentioning my days as a raw foodist would bring back that sense of simpatico I was yearning for.

"I was a raw foodist for an entire year once," I confided.

"Really?" Raw Boy lit up. "Why did you stop?"

The simple mention that I had been a raw foodist put me right back in Raw Boy's good books. I'd pushed the right button, and our whole relationship changed.

"Well, I felt pretty good, but I just couldn't get enough calories. I got really, really skinny until I started eating raw beef. It kept me from withering away, but I got tired of it after about six months."

"What do you mean, you ate raw beef?" Raw Boy demanded.

"I mean I ate a pound of raw cow every day. Mostly rib eyes," I clarified.

"How did you know that was safe?" Raw Boy asked.

"I didn't know. I checked it out the best I could and had to learn from experience. Just like the rest of life."

"Dude, that's insane."

"Not really," I said. "You just make sure to buy quality meat. A good piece of raw beef is just like sushi. Plus, you get tons of B vitamins that get destroyed when you cook the meat, so you feel really alive. But you're right, ultimately you don't know what's going to happen. You just have to pay attention to what happens and go from there. Again, not much different from the rest of life."

"If I wasn't a vegetarian, I'd give it a try," Raw Boy said out of respect for our mutual insanity.

"So my revolutionary morning zinca-mocha-latte program is okay?" I inquired.

"Not what I'd do, but yes, take your zinc with your coffee if you'd like," he said, now smiling as he went to assist another customer, impressed with my raw beef exploits.

"Thank you for your assistance," I replied, as I strolled over to pay for my miraculous prostate-saving supplement.

As I walked out of Henry's to my bicycle, I thought about how my doing what I do tends to provide me with my own little dopamine reward. I get my brain buzz by finding a perspective on a situation where I can see the effortlessness of people doing what they do. I'm pretty sure you don't get a superhero name for merely noticing what is always, already the case, but at least I get a little dopamine from my *way*. Plus, those leotards that go with the superhero capes do look a bit uncomfortable.

I sat on my bike for a moment, and perhaps in a quest for another hit of dopamine, I dropped the entire Rumi bomb on myself:

> *Out beyond ideas of wrongdoing and rightdoing,*
> *there is a field. I'll meet you there.*
> *When the soul lies down in that grass,*
> *the world is too full to talk about.*
> *Ideas, language, and even the phrase each other*
> *doesn't make any sense.*

Ahhh, the full blast of dopamine. I can always find it in that field out beyond rightdoing and wrongdoing, the one where it's clear that everybody is just doing what they do.

Humanity's Insanities

I was still enjoying the high from my Rumi bomb as I pedaled my bike through Henry's parking lot. Everywhere I looked, I saw masters of the human experience. Without even trying, the people all around me were experiencing life in their own unique way. It's hard not to see, once you see it.

My neighbor Nora spotted me as I rode past her car. Being a master in her own right, she naturally did what she does. She called out to me in the voice that is given to all moms upon the birth of their first child. It's the one where they sing a monotone song like they're following a bouncing ball over their own words.

"Wherrrrre's yourrrrr helllllmet?" she called.

"I'mmmm beeeeing carrrreful," I replied.

My use of the extended-enunciation, bouncing-ball voice was technically a violation. I am not a mom and can't legally use it without a permit, but I just couldn't help myself. I had only purchased my bike a few weeks earlier, and it had become clear that the entire world of riding bicycles had changed since I was a child. If I mentioned to anyone that I had recently purchased a bike, their first response was always—and I do mean always—the same.

"You bought a helmet, right?" they would ask.

Initially, I found this reply a bit odd, but then I recalled why society's rules are so tricky: they keep changing all the time. Sometimes it's hard to keep up. I had spent a large portion of my youth going out of my way to severely injure myself on a bicycle. So did all my friends for that matter. We were part of the much-revered Evel Knievel cult. There were millions of members, ninety-nine percent of which were young boys. We would spend hours "borrowing" scrap plywood and scavenging the neighborhood for products to build bicycle ramps, the engineering of which was *very* suspect.

We set the ramps up at various locations depending on what appealed to us that day. The neighborhood creek was always popular. It was the childhood equivalent of Evel Kneivel's failed Snake River jump. The success or failure of our attempts to jump the creek depended on many factors. The structure of the ramp often broke down, but most frequently the physics of the situation had been severely miscalculated despite our advanced fourth-grade math skills. We usually embedded our little bodies, in one way or another, on the opposite bank or in the muddy bottom of the creek. The constant failures never seemed to dampen our enthusiasm.

Of course, when we were bored with creek jumping, we would lie in a row like toy soldiers and jump over each other by way of the same substandard ramp. The distance we would lie from the ramp was continually extended until someone crashed their bike, landed on someone, or both. If the injured party only ran home crying, an executive meeting was held to determine if the stunts should continue. If someone went to the emergency room for stitches, then all additional stunt work was usually canceled for that day. If it was determined that more than three stitches were needed and/or the injured party was diagnosed with a concussion, the parent corporation would often suspend all ramp-related activities for up to a week.

Not once, not ever, not even a single time, did a parent even suggest that someone (anyone) put on a helmet for safety purposes. I know exactly what would have happened. First, everyone would have busted a gut laughing. Then when the moms in the neighborhood realized that this crazy person wasn't kidding (the moms ran the neighborhood), some other mom would have run to the phone and called the cops.

"Quick, send over the guys in the white coats," she'd say, "and have them bring a straightjacket. There's a crazy person down here telling our kids to put on helmets when they ride their bikes."

"Helmets? Did you say, helmets?" the dispatcher would reply.

"Yes, helmets," she'd respond. "She must think our kids are astronauts or something. Do you think she's hallucinating?"

"A squad car is on its way, ma'am. Everything will be okay. Just try to remain calm. I can stay on the line until the car arrives, if you'd like."

Back then "helmets" is not what people did, so I ask you now, "How can someone do what they don't do? Especially when they are so busy doing what they do?" The answer is, "They don't. That's not what they do."

No one even thought of wearing a helmet People do what they do because that's what they do, until their awareness is shifted enough that they start doing something else. This whole concept was summed up in the cartoon I saw years ago where a spiritual seeker arrives at the top of a mountain to ask the wise old sage the meaning of life.

"It's all about hairstyles and fashion," the sage tells the seeker.

The cartoon was funny when I first saw it because it was so absurd, but over the years I've come to see how true it is. Fashion and hairstyles are great examples of people doing what they do, until they don't. The rest of life isn't much different.

We do what we do until there's a big enough shift in awareness that a desire to change arises, or until we are forced to change by outside circumstances. Inevitably, some of us do get left behind and miss the shifts that occur along the way. Perhaps my safety barometer was stuck on a setting whose time had passed, but I'm pretty sure that similar children's stunt work was going on all over America when folks my age were growing up. People understood that sometimes having fun is a little dangerous, and sometimes things that are dangerous hurt a bit while you are having fun doing them. When you are having a dirt bomb fight at the residential construction site, it hurts when you get hit, but I can't think of anything more fun for a ten-year-old boy.

Nowadays, *no helmets* is just not what parents allow their kids to do. It's safety first, safety second, and safety third. The parents are merely doing what they do, and as always, I'm captivated by it. Helmets, car seats, full-body flak jackets for Frisbee, and eye goggles while playing checkers, all "just in case."

When I was four years old, my dad would let me stand on the front passenger seat of the car with the window fully rolled down. As he drove down the road, I would put my hands on the door and stick my head out the window (yes, like a dog). Can you imagine how many tickets my father would get today if a policeman saw me doing that? I'm sure the officer wouldn't understand. Even if my dad explained that it was perfectly safe because he had one finger in my belt loop, it's just not *what is* anymore. That bouncing ball of life keeps on moving.

I've tried to explain to the average bicycle helmet Nazi that when I ride my bike, it's completely different for me than for most cyclists. First of all, I ride my bicycle; I'm not a cyclist. I ride my bike to actually go somewhere, and I'm usually wearing jeans and a t-shirt. I'm not in my shiny spandex shirt and fancy pants riding three across on a two-lane road. You know, the kind of cyclist drivers actually want to hit (subconsciously of course). Oh, and if you happen to be one of these cyclists, then I have no doubt that drivers are actually thrilled with your individual presence on the roadways. You would be the exception that proves the rule.

I pedaled my bike out of the parking lot and glided about a quarter mile down the hill to stop at my bank. I've walked into my bank a thousand times, so I wasn't paying too close attention to my surroundings as I assessed the magnitude of my deposit and its affect on the nation's GNP. I arrived at the front doors and reached for the handle.

"Back off. I said back off. I can get it," a male voice growled.

As I looked down and to my left, I met the scowl of a man in a wheelchair. He assumed I was not going into the bank, but that I had only reached for the door to assist him. I stepped back and allowed him to struggle with the door as he had requested. After he was through the doors, I went straight into the teller line. He ended up directly behind me after stopping at the little bank counter with the pens that don't work. Our eyes met as he pulled up behind me and neither of us said a word.

"I thought you were treating me like a cripple," his facial expression said.

"Nope, I'm going to the bank, just like you," my facial expression replied.

The funny thing is, I do tend to open doors for all types of people: young, old, male, female, the strong and the weak. I especially appreciate it when they don't even acknowledge me with a nod or a thank you. Then I really feel like I've been of service. By taking even less, I feel I've actually given more. It's a math thing.

Each time I stand in line at my bank, I watch as the departing customers are seduced by the front doors. About every third person trying to exit the bank pulls on the handle before they figure out the door needs to be pushed in order to open. If the bank would simply put a flat metal piece where the handle was, one hundred percent of people would push the door because that would be both the intuitive option and the only option. Obsessing about functional door design is apparently not what people do at this branch, which overall is probably a good thing. It gives me something to do as I wait in line, which I appreciate.

As I went to exit the bank, I thought I would save the woman behind me the potential humiliation of pulling on a push door. I passed through the door at normal speed, but then executed a perfect pirouette that left me standing as a sentry holding the door open. The woman behind me had intended to push the door herself, but found nothing but a warm desert breeze to meet the palm of her extended hand. I stood as a humble servant, in perfect harmony with gravity, and allowed her to pass unencumbered.

Her inertia had caused her to pass through the opened door involuntarily, and to my surprise, she turned to examine the person who had tricked her. Her fitted tweed jacket and stern jaw line made her look as though she had spent the morning shushing people at the public library. My new friend, Master Tweedy, couldn't help but inform me of the crime against humanity I had just committed. With two raised eyebrows she let me have it.

"That's sexist, you know."

I was truly not expecting the gift of another lesson from the simple act of opening a door. With masters appearing so frequently in my life, you'd think I'd get used to it, but I never do. I gave her a warm smile and blessed her with a little humor.

"Well, thank you. It is kind of sexy, isn't it? Chivalry is not dead yet."

"I said *ist*, sex*ist*, not *sexy*," she snapped in the tone of a drill sergeant. I braced myself for "You are one stupid son of a bitch, aren't you?" but it never came.

"Ah, all the better then, fair lady. Thank you for your attention to detail."

"Do you even understand what I'm saying?" she asked in frustration.

"I suppose that depends on what *exactly* you are saying."

"I'm saying it is sex*ist* to treat a woman like she is less than you by offering to help her when you wouldn't do the same for a man."

"What do you mean by *less*?" I asked. "I've always felt that the one performing the act of service would be less, since they are giving of themselves."

I didn't want to spoil all the fun and mention that I help all sorts of people all the time because I can't help it. I was an Eagle Scout, and that conditioning doesn't die easily.

"What I mean is that treating someone as though she is different, just because she is a woman, is sexist." Her voice had shifted to a much softer, "I'm sorry, you actually are an idiot" tone.

The lesson was deepening, so I took another bite at the bait the master was laying before me.

"What *exactly* are you implying?"

"To treat a person differently because of their gender is sexist," Master Tweedy instructed.

The masters I encounter each day do seem to revel in the conveyance of their lessons, so I wanted to make sure the teaching wasn't ultimately the opposite of what was being presented.

"So for a man to treat a woman like she is different from a man is sexist?" I clarified.

"Yes. Men need to stop acting so superior. Think about how much more peaceful a place the world would be if women got a chance to run things."

Seconds earlier I was struck by Master Tweedy's range; now it was her depth. She was presenting me with a paradox. The experiencing of a paradox is something I enjoy immensely. The dopamine release in my brain gave me a big lift, and deep inside my cranium, my amygdala was now tying the image of Master Tweedy to that feeling. I couldn't help but have the deepest admiration for her. Her emotional dexterity was very stimulating.

"So if you claim women would do things differently from men, doesn't that mean there are differences between men and women?" I asked, not wanting to miss the lesson.

I sensed that Master Tweedy was pleased with the depth of my insight, but she hid it well. As is the way of all true masters, she immediately tested my understanding again.

"The only difference between men and women is that women happen to be more evolved than men."

"So, there are no differences between men and woman," I began, "except for those differences where women are better than men. Yet somehow, men have been able to oppress women for thousands of years?"

"Yes, that's it. Exactly," she confirmed.

The teaching complete, she turned and marched toward her car, never to gaze upon me again. I stood silently for quite some time, bearing in mind the lesson, a Zen koan really.

Sexism is certainly not pleasant for anyone to experience, but I guess it all depends on how you define it. Master Tweedy was definitely doing what she does, and like everyone else, doing it exceptionally well. Ultimately, I realized it was just another demonstration of the principle: *People do what they do. That's what they do. And* that *is it.* I silently thanked her for taking time out of her busy schedule for me. She certainly was a giver.

Master Tweedy sped away, driving as well as any man, I might add, and I thought to myself how crazy we all are. I do think that if we could all just raise our right hands and say out loud, "I hereby state that I'm certifiably crazy, nuts, outta-da-box insane, but I'm doing the best I can with it, so cut me a little slack," the world would be a better place.

Perhaps I grasp the insanity of people more easily than others because I grew up in a small home with seven family members all sharing one bathroom: two parents, three older sisters, me, and one younger brother. Each child was two years apart. This gave my mother a very generous recovery time after giving birth before she got knocked up again with the next kid. Most mothers in the neighborhood got about three months off between labor and re-insemination, so my mom was apparently living the life of Riley.

All seven of us living under a fairly small roof did tend to magnify the idiosyncrasies of human behavior. So much so, that I couldn't help but be branded with certain lessons. When all my sisters were teenagers, my brother and I realized that about every four weeks the women in our home pretty much went crazy. At this time, men became the enemy to be hunted and then filleted whenever possible.

"You pick the topic, and we'll fight about it," the females would say to the three testosterone-laden humans in the house (I'm paraphrasing here a bit).

Like the rest of life, it can be shocking when you don't understand what's going on, but once you get it, you just deal with things accordingly. My brother and I decided that at approximately twenty-eight-day intervals, it would be wise to spend a lot of time away from home for a few days. We also concluded that it would be *fun* to camp in the backyard in the musty tent my dad had purchased on a whim years earlier.

Upon getting the tent home, my dad most likely realized that camping would probably turn out like the attempt to deep-fry the Thanksgiving turkey. It would be a total disaster that the rest of the family would not even be allowed to mention in his presence. The tent was quickly approaching the unmentionable zone, so my dad was just happy it was being used.

My brother and I would be going along with our lives when there would be a vague sense that something was "off" with the women in the house. One of us would be like Radar O'Reilly on the television show *M.A.S.H.* and say the equivalent of "I hear choppers." The other brother would inevitably respond, "I don't hear anything," and then within moments, one of my sisters would start bitching at us because our hearts were beating too loudly or our eyes were the wrong color.

Sometimes my brother and I would be so distracted by constant skirmishes that it wasn't until we'd see a tampon wrapper in the basket that we'd figure it out.

"Incoming!" one of us would scream, and we could have the tent set up and fully stocked within twenty minutes. Time is everything when lives hang in the balance.

This monthly avoidance tactic worked well until the winter months in New England came around. Camping in a canvas tent with cheap polyester sleeping bags in the middle of February is, to say the least, overrated. Thus, it was Mother Nature herself who forced me into realizing humanity's insanities as the basis of all human existence.

I was thirteen when the famous Blizzard of '78 struck. About four feet of snow landed on us in less than twenty-four hours. No school. No work. Only emergency vehicles were allowed on the roads. And all four women in my home were simultaneously PMSing.

"Let the games begin," was all I could think at the time. I had no idea this would be an opportunity for intense learning and deep spiritual insight.

No matter where I went in my home, an estrogen-enhanced master teacher would seek me out and begin poking and prodding me to test the depth of my understanding. At first I made the classic mistake of trying to soothe the savage sages with reasonable and sincere explanations for things. It was obvious to all that my level of understanding was superficial at best. Throwing rationality into such a vortex of emotion was just tossing chum into the water for the sharks. It only whets their appetites for more.

There is an old Taoist saying, "Never wrestle with a pig. You both get muddy, and the pig likes it." By day three, the PMS squad had frustrated me past the point of resisting any longer. I could wrestle no more. I was exhausted, a beaten thirteen-year-old man. I decided that my sisters and my mother were all absolutely crazy, so I might as well just agree with whatever they said.

My mother appeared in the living room, took a deep inhale, and spoke the following words in a single breath: "I'm very disappointed in you. I thought if I didn't say anything, you would read my mind and know that I really would have appreciated you shoveling our driveway with the eight-foot snowdrifts and ignore the fact that the snowplow will only deposit more snow in the driveway when it plows the street. And even though I can't drive anywhere with the four feet of snow covering every single street in New England, you should begin shoveling toward Boston instead of sitting there watching TV because I think that might make me feel better." I'm paraphrasing here, of course.

"You're right, Mom," I replied, "I'm sorry I didn't think to do that. Would you mind if I volunteered to make shoveling the driveway my sole responsibility? That way you don't have to worry about it at all."

Her brain cramped at my response.

"Okay," she murmured, and then walked away.

I felt like I had discovered kryptonite. The anti-crazy serum had finally been discovered and could be easily administered in a little capsule called, "offer no resistance."

A few moments later, I came out of the lone bathroom in the house after taking an entire three minutes to conclude my business.

"You *always* take *forever* in the bathroom," my sister barked.

"You're right. I'll try to be more considerate in the future."

That was all I offered her. She stopped dead in her tracks, not knowing what to do next. I had given her nothing to sink her teeth into. The sea of estrogen miraculously parted before me, and I peacefully went on my way.

Two hours after that, another master teacher accused me of never cleaning my dirty dishes. In complete harmony with the principle, I agreed with her.

"You are absolutely right. From now on, I'm really going to do my best to always wash my dishes before I leave the kitchen."

She stood silently with no idea of what to do next. I was a cul-de-sac that turned her back toward herself. From that moment on I viewed the PMS interactions with my female family members as mini self-improvement seminars that they were kind enough to provide free of charge. Their cyclical generosity could never again be overlooked. This understanding, which began as the very small PMS Principle, eventually became the Humanity's Insanities Principle. I eventually realized that it wasn't just PMSing women who are crazy—*everybody* is crazy. It's just that sometimes it's more obvious than others.

It wasn't a long drive to realize the males in our home were just as crazy as the women; it was a very short putt. When it came to yard work, why would we think it made sense that the boys deal with everything that is green and brown, and the women deal with everything that has color? These were the actual rules for yard work at our house. It kind of made sense, sort of, but we kids probably spent more time arguing about the rule than actually doing yard work. We certainly could have used Master Tweedy back then to declare all yard work to be asexual.

As my understanding deepened, there were many observations of each gender's insanity, along with each family's unique brand of crazy. For example, as a generality, but by no means an absolute, it was interesting to me that the most prized possessions of the women in our house tended to be fragile, expensive, and non-utilitarian; and the most prized possessions of the males seemed to be durable, inexpensive, and utilitarian. The family drama that ensued when someone accidentally broke my sister's glass horse still lives on in infamy, but when that same sister knowingly ruined my jack knife by dismantling a birdhouse I had built, all was forgiven. After all, she wanted the wood for an art project, so I was ordered to just get over it.

We're all crazy, and once you realize everyone is nuts, life is much less frustrating. Then all that remains is a simple fascination with it all.

While walking to my bike outside the bank I glanced over to see Master Tweedy run a red light. The six cameras at the intersection all flashed. They had captured an image of her face and her license plate. A traffic ticket would be in the mail to her the next day. This was photographic evidence that she did in fact drive just as recklessly as any man—proof positive of our mutual insanity.

I hopped on my bike and looked around at all the people as I rode. I could see crazy everywhere: the guy keeping everyone in line waiting because he's too busy talking on his cell phone to do his transaction, the sports fan on the TV in the store window thinking that it matters one jot if his team wins, the homeowner at the next store obsessing about new fixtures and paint swatches, even the fat homeless person on the sidewalk with a sign that says, "Need money for food." The old, the young, and the in-betweens: all crazy.

If you step back and take a look, everybody is a complete nut-job. This single realization about humanity helps the experience of living make a lot more sense. The females in my childhood home, the guy in the wheelchair, Master Tweedy, *me*, and virtually anyone you meet will give you a glimpse of the insanity we call humanity. We are all masters of our own delusions moving through the world, projecting our lens of reality onto everyone else. It's not that hard to see. All you have to do is look, and not even that much.

O-Ring People

I was home from the bank for about ten minutes when the doorbell rang. By now I'm sure you can understand my excitement, as my memory banks were full of enchanting experiences that had begun with the simple act of opening a door.

I have noticed that the ringing of a doorbell doesn't tend to elicit the same type of reaction in others. My neighbor has a sign on his door that depicts a more common point of view. It reads "To Solicitors: Before knocking, please remove rings, watches, belt buckles, and other metal objects. Our pit bull has trouble digesting such items. Thank you for your cooperation." It's a bit over the top for me, but my neighbor got a kick out of it when I joked with him about the idea. That's why I typed it up and had it laminated for him to put on his door. It seemed like the neighborly thing to do.

Doorknockers of all types are welcome at my home, even when their intentions are questionable. Just a week earlier a somewhat pudgy teenager knocked on my door with less than admirable goals. I found our interaction to be enjoyable, and I think we both learned something from the exchange.

"Hi, my name is Peter," he said, speaking rapidly. "My Mom is Carol. We live a few streets over. You probably know her; she's the one who has the crafts parties."

"No, I don't know her," I replied.

"Oh, well, I'm sure you got the flyer I put in your mailbox the other day about our soccer team raising money to go play in England."

"No, I didn't get any flyers. Where do you live?"

"Just a few streets over," he said, with a vague wave of his hand indicating that he lived somewhere in the Western Hemisphere. "My soccer team is trying to raise money to go play in Europe."

He was just doing what he does, so I figured I would just do what I do.

"Yes, you already said that. What's the name of the street you live on?" I inquired.

He began to fidget, and his eyes darted about in all directions. I was worried he might be having a seizure, but then in the tone of game show contestant, he took a wild guess. "Uh, Beechtree?"

He sensed that I was onto his scam, but he was still willing to continue despite the mounting odds against him. I found his professionalism and commitment to excellence admirable.

"Beechtree is this street," I said. "So you live on this street?"

"Ah, yeah," he muttered.

"What number?" I asked.

"What?"

He sighed at the excessive effort I was causing him to exert. I could almost hear him thinking, "You mean there's more questions? Being a con man is more work than I thought."

"What's the street number of your home?" I asked, "The one you live in with your mother."

"Ummmmm, 285?" he offered, like he was guessing how many jellybeans were in a jar.

I think we could both appreciate that he had made it to the Double Jeopardy round of the game, so I'm sure he figured he might as well take a shot. The problem for him was that I lived at 221 Beechtree, and the street was only a half-mile long.

"Oh, 285 is right down the street," I offered. "I'll tell you what, let's go down to your house so I can meet your mom, and then I'll give you twenty bucks toward your trip."

"Sounds good," he said with an I'll-show-you kind of confidence.

After all, it was a bit insulting for me to be questioning the validity of his heartwarming story. Apparently I had not read the latest federal notice that anything "for the children" was beyond questioning.

As I bent down to grab my shoes, the young lad spun on a dime and began fleeing at a dead sprint. By the time my bare feet reached the end of the walkway, he was three houses away and going strong. As I reached the end of my driveway, he was turning the corner and headed out of the neighborhood.

"Wow, pretty fast for such a pudgy guy," I thought to myself. "I wonder what position he plays on the soccer team."

A week had passed since the con man. I now opened the door to find three Jehovah's Witnesses. They had come to save my soul from eternal damnation, which I thought was pretty nice, all things considered.

Religious solicitors of all kinds were common in my neighborhood, but at the moment it was the witnesses of Jehovah whose presence I was being blessed with. There was a Jehovah's Witness church (think Christians with no Christmas) about a mile away. They were sandwiched between a Greek Orthodox church (think funny square black hats) and a Jewish temple (think little hats to cover male pattern baldness). The Mormons (think Utah and blonde; or for those in the know, think funny underwear) were a mile in the other direction. They were right next to the Catholic church (no, don't think that; think tall pointy hat riding in the Popemobile). One street over from me, in the cross hairs of all these different groups, was the Church of Religious Science (I'm pretty sure you can think whatever you want).

The soul savers of the community seemed to be the Jehovahs, the Mormons, and the Born Agains. I'm not sure where the Born Agains' church was. They would just miraculously appear out of nowhere. Hmm, maybe that's something worth looking into?

All the soul savers seemed pretty nice. The Mormons were probably on the top of my list because they even offered to do free yard work. I thought that was pretty cool even though I never took them up on it. Plus, the Mormons always wore white button-down shirts with name tags, so you knew immediately who it was. It saved time. That way we could just dive right into all the questions about polygamy.

I was genuinely fascinated with the soul savers when they visited. It's not often that I can just stand there and ask people any questions I want. It's really an unbelievable opportunity, and I seldom passed on a chance to experience it. The circularity of their thinking and the way it was so walled off from any kind of objective or well-reasoned analysis seemed kind of like those O-rings on the space shuttle. They have to be perfectly sealed or the entire thing blows up.

Having three Jehovah's Witnesses standing before me with their Bibles and *The Watchtower* magazines in hand was a bit surprising. They usually traveled in pairs, so this was a special day. One soul saver was usually a veteran of the soul saving arts, and the other was an apprentice of sorts. But today I was being blessed with a middle-aged man who appeared to be the veteran, a young man, and a young woman. The two youngsters seemed to be relatively new to this experience.

"Sir," the young male blurted out, "what do you think of when you see a homeless person pushing a shopping cart down the street?"

When discussing topics like God, the devil, hell, heaven, and anything in the vicinity of eternity, I generally like to know the names of the people I'm speaking with. But the young Jehovah male was in no mood for introductions, so I was left to fend for myself when it came to picking names.

Out of respect, I wanted to think of them biblically. Plus, I thought it might give our discussion the creationist flavor that was so often missing in these dark times. For the two newbie soul savers, naming them after the newbiest couple that ever existed seemed appropriate, so Adam and Eve were my immediate choices.

Veteran soul saver was a bit more difficult. I was going to cop out and go with *Dude*, but I knew there wasn't a single Dude within the entire text of the Bible (not even in Revelation). I realized that my elder Jehovah friend must have been wandering from door to door for years, so I went with the biblical name *Cain*, as Cain was cursed to be a wanderer for mouthing off to God.

The story goes that God had asked Cain the whereabouts of his brother Abel, and Cain just wasn't in the mood.

"Am I my brother's keeper?" Cain wisecracked to God.

Cain saying these few well-chosen words to God (allegedly) was all it took to get him cursed. Personally, I think Cain showed a fair bit of restraint. It could have been much worse.

"You're the one who is always bragging about being all-knowing. Work it out," is what God would have gotten if he'd asked someone from Massachusetts, but I guess that's why they call us Massholes.

With Adam, Eve, and Cain all named, I was ready to answer the question about the guy pushing a shopping cart down the street. The long pause I'd taken in picking names left my audience thirsty for a reply.

"Sometimes," I declared. "With great compassion for that person, I think, 'There, too, is your all-powerful god's handiwork.'"

There was a long pause, so I added, "Then again—shopping twenty-four hours a day—isn't that the American dream? Maybe he's just a small reflection of that all-loving God you folks like to talk about."

I should point out that I look upon these visits from religious folks more like a play date than an attempt to be brainwashed or spiritually seduced. As long as we are all expressing our views honestly, I don't think there's any harm in having a little fun.

I would have gone easy on Adam, but what good was that going to do anyone? So I decided to just give him honest answers. Then he and Cain could discuss what happened later. When it came to Adam mastering his sales pitch, I figured it was no different from selling anything else: trial by fire was the best. Plus, how could my wonderful sense of humor not add a dimension to the conversation that is so often missed in these encounters?

"Have you gotten a chance to read *The Watchtower* magazines we leave at your front door?" Adam continued.

"Yes, I have," I confirmed.

"What do you think after reading them?"

"Honestly, I think you people don't show a great deal of faith."

My statement caused Adam to flinch. His head jolted upward and to the right like a toy rock 'em, sock 'em robot. His eyes darted over to his mentor, but the double-eyebrow raise of Cain said it all: *He's all yours. This is what we're out here for.* Adam untilted his head and gave me an intense stare.

"What do you mean, we lack faith?" he implored.

Remember, I was merely giving honest replies to their queries. They were the ones who had volunteered for my responses by knocking on my door and asking their loaded questions.

"Your magazine is jam-packed with messages of fear and greed. Fear that such-and-such will happen in the future and greed about what you can do now to get your reward later. As far as I can tell, you might as well be selling a gold buyer's investment guide."

"Why would you say that?" Adam inquired.

"Well, you guys claim to believe in an all-powerful god," I replied.

"I do," insisted Adam.

"Well, I'm no Bible scholar, but doesn't Matthew 10:29 say, 'Not a sparrow can fall without it being the will of the Father.' And Matthew 10:30, 'fear not, therefore; you are of more value than many sparrows.' Plus, there's something in there like, 'all the hairs on your head are numbered.'"

"Yes, that's correct," Adam confirmed, but I could tell he wasn't getting my point.

"That Bible you hold in your hand," I said, "Is that the direct word of your god?"

"Yes. Absolutely," Adam asserted.

"Well then, why all the worry? Your book, the direct word of your god, says that nothing can happen without it being the will of your god. So can't you all just relax a bit? According to your book, your god is doing everything."

I stood with my shoulders shrugged and my palms turned upward as I waited for a reply. All three of the soul savers stared silently back at me. In the interest of being a good host, I felt it would be an appropriate time to add a little humor to dissipate some of the tension we'd built, so I dove into one of my favorite jokes:

So, this guy is walking along the side of a one thousand foot cliff. The ground gives way, and he tumbles over the edge. About one hundred feet down he grabs hold of a little branch that is jutting out of the cliff's face. He hangs there, with nothing but rocks nine hundred feet below his dangling body.

"Help! Help! Is anybody up there? Help!" he screams.

After a little while, a booming voice comes out of the sky.

"This is your all-powerful, omnipotent God. I can help, if you'd like."

"Yes, yes. Please help," the man cries.

"Okay, are you ready?" God asks.

"Yes, yes. Please hurry. I can't hold on much longer," the man screams.

"All right, here it is," God's voice booms, "LET GO."

To which the guy hanging from the branch yells, "Is there anybody else up there?"

Nothing. I got absolutely no response from my humor-challenged audience of three. Only blank stares. Perhaps I needed to work on my timing. Comedians always say that timing is the key to getting laughs. It was clear something was off in my presentation.

"My point," I reiterated, "is that if you believe in an all-powerful god, and you believe the words in your book that say everything is the will of your god, then your only job is to be the awareness of each moment, which you already are, so you can just let go."

"But we have the power of free will, sir," Adam replied.

"Ohhhhhhhhhhh," I returned with a playful smile. "So you want it both ways. Now I understand why you're so stressed. You don't get to have both free will and an all-powerful god. That's cheating. And when you try to cheat, you suffer. If you want your free will, then you can only have a *kinda* powerful god. If you have the power to go against your god, then your god is not all-powerful, which is fine if that's the way you want to go."

"Sir, have you found Jesus?" Eve chimed in.

She was hoping to shift the conversation and help out her buddy, Adam, which I appreciated. I went with her question because I'm pretty sure this was a bold move and against the training procedures. She'd taken more than her share of the blame for that whole apple incident in the Garden of Eden, so I didn't want her getting in any more trouble.

"Absolutely. Just last Tuesday, Jesus was cutting my lawn."

I couldn't resist. Every other Spanish-speaking immigrant in this town is named Jesus. I'd been waiting to use that joke for six months, and although it was a bit forced, it felt pretty darn good to get it out of my system.

"I don't mean *that* Jesus," Eve corrected.

I searched for even the slightest hint of amusement in her voice but detected none. This was a tough crowd, but I sensed that I was wearing them down, so I continued with my set.

"Oh, *that* Jesus. I'm pretty sure *that* Jesus is in prison," I said.

"Why would you think Jesus is in prison?" Eve said, swallowing the bait.

"Well that's where lots of folks seem to find him."

I was in the zone. But nothing, not a single laugh from my audience. Not even a smirk. My timing must have been way off.

"If you don't accept Jesus Christ, then you will never be able to experience heaven on earth," Adam asserted.

"I wasn't going to bring this up, but since you put it out there, I have a question. This all-knowing, all-powerful, omniscient, omnipotent (I thought the redundancy would help) god of yours has set it up so *only* those who accept Jesus Christ in your particular way will be allowed to experience heaven. Is that correct?"

"Yes," Eve said, with nods of affirmation from Adam and Cain.

"So your all-knowing, all-powerful god who knows the past, present, and future of all things has basically predetermined that the vast majority of people throughout history will not 'accept Jesus.' Your all-powerful god has basically predetermined that the vast majority of people in the world will be damned to burn and suffer in hell for all eternity. And your god set the whole thing up this way on purpose. Is that correct?"

"Yes," came from both Adam and Eve. An arrogant nod was the only response from Cain (this guy definitely mouthed off to God).

Fascinating, I thought to myself. Then I was struck in the gut with a feeling that all four of us were secretly hoping for more of my humor. I'm very intuitive that way, so I just dove right in with the following joke:

So this guy dies and meets St. Peter at the Pearly Gates. After brief introductions and confirmation of his reservation, St. Peter takes the new arrival on a tour of heaven.

"Over there is our Eskimo population doing all their Eskimo stuff," said St. Peter as they strolled through the grounds. "Up here is our Hindu population doing all the things that Hindus do."

St. Peter continued the tour and at a certain point turned to the man and said, "I need you to be very quiet as we walk past this cement wall."

The man complied with St. Peter's request as they both tiptoed past the wall, but after they were a good distance away, the man asked, "St. Peter, I could hear all sorts of goings on, on the other side of that wall. Why did we need to be so quiet?"

To which St. Peter replied, "Because those are the Jehovah's Witnesses. They think they are the only ones here."

My timing was perfect, the joke was on topic, and I'm pretty sure none of them had heard it before. Yet, after a perfectly placed punch line, I got nothing but blank stares. *Absolutely fascinating*, was the thought that kept rising in my mind. These folks are thrilling to spend time with. I could stand here all day chatting with them.

I waited and waited and waited, but all three soul savers were speechless. Not even a snide remark from wisecracking Cain. I eventually had to face the fact that, perhaps, my humor had an effect opposite from what I had intended. Life will surprise you.

As the host, I decided a new question was in order, one that my guests might be truly enthusiastic about.

"Just so we're clear," I began, "you guys believe that Jesus was the son of God, was born of a virgin, was crucified and died for the sins of mankind, and rose from the dead three days later. Is that about right?"

"Yes, that's correct," said Cain, obviously feeling more comfortable now that the conversation was back on track.

"And you guys believe that virgin births, dying for the sins of all others, and coming back from the dead are all possible?" I asked.

"Yes, we do," all three responded in harmony (actually, Adam was a bit flat).

"Okay, so it only makes sense that you guys would also believe in Krishna, the godman from India, fourteen hundred years *before* Jesus, who was born of a virgin, was crucified and died for everyone's salvation, who rose from the dead and ascended into heaven. Oh, and lastly, he's supposed to come back to judge the living and the dead, which should also sound a bit familiar."

"No, we only believe in Jesus Christ," Eve replied.

"But don't you find it interesting that basically the same story was being celebrated somewhere else in the world fourteen hundred years before your story even existed?" I asked.

"I don't know anything about Krishna," Cain said in a tone that was so sarcastic I could begin to understand why God had cursed him.

"Seriously, forget the guys with the shaved heads and orange robes jumping up and down chanting on the sidewalk. And forget the fact that Krishna was blue like Papa Smurf. I'm talking about the historical fact that practically the identical story of Jesus existed in India over a thousand years before your Jesus existed. As a matter of fact, the Egyptians had the godman Horus with a virtually identical story to Jesus, thousands of years before your Jesus. And the Persians had the godman Mythra, again with the same story, long before your Jesus. I mean, can you really be sure you guys are the only horse in the race, or is it just possible that there might be more than just one way?"

Adam and Eve seemed genuinely intrigued by the points I was making. Their eyes were wide open, as were their mouths. Their heads slowly nodding, as happens when you really connect with someone. Finally, we were getting down to some real discussion.

"That's very interesting," Eve granted.

"And even if your Jesus is *one* of the ways, it seems to me you folks are worshiping the teapot instead of drinking the tea," I said. "If you believe in an all-powerful god, then all of this, right here, right now, all the time, is God. This experiencing right now is God. Maybe that's what Jesus meant when he said that he was God?"

"Hmmm," came the audible sound from Eve's lips.

Cain saw that we were beginning to reach a place of agreement and took the opportunity to dive in with his own opinion. With great authority and conviction he looked down at his watch and nodded his head. "Well, we really need to get to another appointment. Thank you for your time."

"Thank you for your time," Adam and Eve echoed.

Cain then gently placed his hands on the upper backs of his two trainees, right between the shoulder blades. It appears that this is where the controls were found because all three turned in a synchronistic move that looked like it came from some ancient pagan ritual. It was like the Rockettes, but without the kicking.

It was interesting to me that the pressing appointment my Jehovah friends needed to get to had come on so suddenly, but I do appreciate that there are a lot of souls to save. Also, I guess even soul savers have a limit. I'm sure my address is now on the do-not-darken-this-guy's-door list. I can only hope they share their information with the telemarketers.

They walked away much more slowly than the con man the week before. I found Adam, Eve, and Cain to be a bewitching little coven. Our conversation stayed with me long after I closed the door. Then again, I've always been impressed with any well-developed cognitive dissonance. These folks must have the strength of Sampson to sustain such a wall of denial in the face of all reasonable perspectives on what they purport to believe.

I realized long ago that I just don't have the flexibility to perform the mental gymnastics required to prop up their religious views. I'm sure I would pull a hamstring if I even tried. How could I not be impressed with the intensity of their commitment? I do think my sense of humor made an impression on them as well. Of course I didn't use all the arrows in my quiver. I didn't even go with, "If we're all God's children, why is Jesus so special?" I figured I'd save that one for next time.

I also knew that any stress I had created in the soul savers had caused their adrenal glands to spit a bit of cortisol into their systems.

They were now discussing the Bible passages that proved beyond the shadow of a doubt that my perspectives were completely and utterly wrong. I knew that my opinions were currently being diluted and mixed with what they already knew to be true. A surge of dopamine was being released as a reward for the reinforcement of their previously established way of thinking.

In short, that little kick of dopamine would be mixed with the cortisol that had been released moments before. The cortisol-dopamine cocktail that ensued would probably be the best high they get all day. As we all know, the resolution of something negative in our lives can provide a tremendous rush. If you've ever lost your wallet and then found it, you know the joy of just getting back to even.

The self-mixed biochemical cocktail in their bodies would also deepen the beliefs that they project onto the world, which is the whole point of trying to convert others. It's about deepening their own faith, not yours, but I'm sure at some level we're all aware of that. Even if the only result of our time together was the good feeling that comes from supersealing the O-rings of their belief system, it was a great play date. Plus, at some deep level, I'm sure they took comfort in the fact that I'm just the way their all-powerful god made me.

Oh, I almost forgot to point to the obvious fact that we're all O-ring people. It's just that most folks are more covert about it than the soul savers. We all have a little lawyer in our head who is ready to confabulate a story that denies points against our side and forcefully magnifies those points in our favor—for the good of the client, of course. This O-ring tendency of the human species is the basis of most political feuds, family feuds, relationship feuds, and of course, religious feuds.

"Go forth and confabulate," seems to be humanity's divine order. Have you confabulated today?

The Wonder of What-Is-ing

My play date with the Jehovahs left me famished from all the mental exercise. It had turned into quite a workout. Since your brain burns about 20 percent of your calories, I thought the Jehovahs might want to consider wearing calorie counter displays around their necks like the ones on a treadmill. Think about it—even if a pagan wasn't particularly interested in discussing *The Watchtower* magazine, they just might endure the soul-saving sales pitch until they hit the 350- or 400-calorie mark. The potential converts would get to burn calories, and the Jehovahs would get to reinforce their own beliefs. It could be a real win-win.

I was soon in my backyard, eating my regular lunch of a turkey and cranberry sauce sandwich. I am often amused at how I still love the cranberry sauce I ate as a child. If it doesn't have the molded rings on it from the can it came out of, it's just not for me. I also had a piece of my favorite desert, *tres leches* cake, set aside to end my lunch on a note of sweet perfection.

Tres leches translates as "three milks." It's basically a butter cake soaked in sweetened condensed milk, evaporated milk, and cream. It's also one of the best things to ever meet my taste buds. The first time I tried tres leches at my local Peruvian restaurant, El Q'ero, was much like the internal orgasms one has when doing tantric yoga, except it didn't take ninety minutes. Actually, forget about the calorie counter idea for the Jehovahs. They should just hand strangers a piece of tres leches. I'm pretty sure people would listen to anything with a tres leches bribe, although the Jehovahs might end up with a rather chubby congregation.

I took a moment to enjoy the unique flavor of my candied cranberry sauce and recalled that I've always had very distinct preferences in sandwiches. It's truly amazing what your brain will do with such a thought. Mine did a search for all the memory files that had *sandwich* associated with them. I didn't even ask it to; brains are proactive that way.

There was a flash of the power-packed brown sugar and margarine sandwich on white bread from my childhood, along with the marmalade sandwiches Mrs. Olney used to make me. I'm pretty sure there was an image of a meatball sub from my youth, and then maybe a turkey and avocado sandwich from Togo's in my twenties. My brain finished up with a shot of me back as young child eating a sandwich at the beach.

My view of life has been very affected by sand was the next thought that my brain offered up. You see, when I was three or four years old, I used to like to dip my peanut butter and jelly sandwiches in the sand when my family went to the beach. I liked how it made my sandwich crunchy. I can still see the sand-coated white bread and the unique crunchy granules mixed into the peanut butter and jelly.

The physical sensation of sand between your teeth is singular and not soon forgotten.

The discovery of sand as a condiment was kind of like those Reese's Peanut Butter Cup commercials where the peanut butter and chocolate somehow crash into each other and a wonderful discovery is made. I'm pretty sure I just dropped my sandwich, like all little kids do at the beach, and a well-meaning sibling intuitively knew I would enjoy the crunchiness added by the sand. No doubt one of my sisters was kind enough to encourage me to eat the sand-coated sandwich that others would have wasted.

I could claim we kids were all brainwashed not to waste food with the guilt-inducing line about the starving children in China, India, or Africa that parents everywhere seem to use. Apart from the fact that every kid knows the food on their plate would never get to those poor children, that line was never used in my house. There was a simple reason as to why. Do the math, as they say. Add up the grocery bill for two adults and five growing children and then subtract it from the blue collar salary of a telephone man, and there's not a lot left over. If you didn't clean your plate in my house, my father did.

"Are you gonna eat that?" my dad would ask as he eyed the food on your plate. If you didn't give a strong and rapid "Yes," it was gone.

Back at the beach of my childhood, I was the fourth of my mother's five children. She was done obsessing over what her children put in their mouths. That was for child one and maybe child two. By the time I came along, anything that would not cause permanent organ damage or block my ability to breathe was fine. Although gum off the sidewalk was still discouraged.

Until I was six or seven years old, every time we went to the beach I would have my sand-dipped sandwiches, I have a much closer relationship with sand than most. I don't think it actually worked its way into my DNA, and I'd even be surprised if any of those original grains are stuck in my body somewhere. It's probably just the fondness for the sandwiches of my youth, the joyful memories of those grains of sand between my teeth, that stuck in my memory banks in a way that makes me pay attention to sand in ways others do not.

My fifth-grade field trip to the Boston Museum of Science serves as a prime example of the resonance that sand and I share, and the lessons I learn from being around it. There aren't many greater highs for a child than a field trip during school hours. Sixty screaming little lunatics jumped off the school bus ready to storm the building. We were milling around before we charged into the museum when my teacher, Miss Reeves, spotted a tough-looking Italian kid smoking a cigarette. He was standing a few yards away, on the other side of a chain link fence, when Miss Reeves marched over to him. I could tell he was no more than eleven years old because he couldn't quite grow a full beard yet.

"Young man," she barked. "Put that cigarette out and tell me what school you are supposed to be attending while you are out here lollygagging around."

All the kids from my class were from a small town where anyone's mom or a teacher is given respect, regardless of whether you know them personally. It was a conspiracy all the adults were in on. It seemed to work pretty well, so none of us could have imagined what happened next.

This future member of La Cosa Nostra looked up at Miss Reeves and sent a steady stream of smoke out of the left side of his Popeye-shaped mouth. He assessed the worthiness of his opponent for a full second with a cocky survey of Miss Reeves from head to toe. Then with a style I've yet to *ever* witness again, he let her have it.

"Lick my ass, bitch," he snapped.

When he said "bitch," he head-butted the air in front of him. It was clear that this wasn't the first time he had ever said those choice words. He then turned his back on Miss Reeves and casually strolled across the basketball court and into the adjoining park.

From start to finish, the event displayed a disregard and lack of respect that was mindblowing. We kids were so shocked that no one could even laugh. Not only would none of us have ever dared to do such a thing, we never would have even *thought* of doing it. It was so far out of our world of possibility that our little brains could barely believe it happened. And even if we had thought to do such a thing, we certainly would never have used the precise and vivid phrasing that our little mafioso friend had applied.

There were questions consuming my entire brain (reptilian, limbic, and prefrontal cortex; conscious, subconscious, and superconscious): *Where on earth does a kid like that come from? How would he ever think he could get away with that?* and *How did he actually get away with it?* It's obvious that he had the system all worked out. I now realize his smoking was probably a calculated move to be one of the future multimillion-dollar tobacco lawsuit winners.

The incident with Miss Reeves and the lollygagger stayed with me for quite a while. By the time I got to the second floor of the museum, I had expelled much of the adrenaline-induced mania from the incident and was back to a reasonably calm state of mind.

I was with a small group of kids that came upon a wave machine. It was basically some blue jelly in a ten-foot-long rectangular box that tipped back and forth like a seesaw. It was spellbinding. I stayed until I was the only one left in front of the wave machine and walked back and forth as each wave formed and broke in slow motion. After ten minutes, I was completely tranced out by the whole experience.

The rest of the kids were at displays that showed how gears worked or how water seeks its own level, but I wandered over to a display on human overpopulation. It had you stand in a three foot by three foot square and claimed that this is how much space you would have to live in if everyone didn't stop having so many children. I think they said that if everyone didn't stop having sex within something like twenty minutes, it would be too late.

The message was simple: you'll have three square feet to live in, so stop having babies. At the time it seemed that whether this turned out to be a good thing or a bad thing would depend a lot on who your neighbors were. It might not be too bad if I were sandwiched between Sandra Sincero and Celeste Marchetti, the two hot girls in my class. I guess I had a thing for Italian girls. The display was obviously very effective because I've still got a bit of elbowroom out here in California.

I shook off the effects of the doomsday population display and walked on until I noticed a bucket sized metal funnel hanging from a chain. The point was to fill the funnel with sand and give it a good shove. You could then watch the designs it made on the platform below as it swung around and emptied out. I did this for a while and, as with the wave machine, I got a bit of a rush from the buoyancy of a light trance state.

I was obviously a bit of a trance junkie. In my altered state I started thinking about Miss Reeves and the lollygagger. I contemplated the inevitable overpopulation I was about to experience in the very near future and how we're all going to be squished together someday like the grains of sand, all jammed together in the funnel of life.

"Would you like to see something neat?" a voice behind me asked.

I turned to find a geeky guy with thick black glasses pointing at the funnel. He seemed genuinely excited about teaching me some science. I figured either he worked at the museum or was some MIT student. Back then, we hadn't been taught to be wary of the "admirers of children" in the world, so I felt pretty safe.

"Sure, go ahead," I replied.

He cleared the platform of sand with a big brush, filled the funnel, and let it empty out on one spot. While it emptied, he kept shoveling up more sand from the sides of the platform and dumping it into the top of the funnel. It made a single pile of sand that kept building and collapsing, again and again. *Boring,* I thought to myself. But Mr. Science had a very interesting point.

"If we continually filled this funnel," he said, "scientists could tell us pretty accurately how many times an hour this pile of sand will build on itself and then collapse. But they can never tell us exactly when it will collapse or exactly how it will collapse. There are too many variables. Each grain of sand affects the others in so many different ways that we can never calculate them all."

I stood and watched the pile of sand build and collapse, again and again. I knew something about it was important. I stood there for quite a while. My little abstracting mind just loved the interplay of all those grains of sand and the idea that an esoteric life lesson might be culled from it.

After a while, I wandered over and looked down at the huge T-Rex skeleton from the hole in the second floor. Then I walked along and examined a timeline of Earth's 4.5 billion-year history and read how humans had only been here for one hundred thousand of them. I read how we've been here "way less" than one percent of the time the earth has been here and thought about how big the number 4.5 billion was. I'll only be here for approximately seventy years; in the big scheme of things that's not too much. That was the lesson I took away.

In later years I learned that "scientific Adam" was the one male we can all trace our genetic ancestry to. He lived sixty thousand years ago in the Rift Valley in Kenya. Scientific Adam was a black man. It was only after the glaciers receded fifty thousand years ago that people migrated out of Africa and developed different-colored skin and body types. That's why on any survey that asks me to declare my race, I generally check the box for African American. If they don't specify, I go with the science.

Anyway, I checked out a whole bunch of other exhibits at the museum, but the sand was in the back of my mind. It was important. That kid who said, "Lick my ass, bitch" was important, too. I don't know why, but I just kept bearing in mind that pile of sand building and collapsing, again and again. Then occasionally the little lollygagger would rise to the top of my thoughts as well.

On the way home, my friends Pinky and Packy were engaged in an innocent spitball fight when something went terribly wrong. One of the saliva soaked projectiles accidentally lodged in Mr. Bodellini's beard. He was an innocent chaperone and it was the final of many transgressions that had already occurred on the trip. It required a strong and immediate disciplinary response. We all knew it. When the entire bus was sentenced to sit in total silence for the last thirty minutes of the bus ride back to school, we gracefully accepted our fate. None would dare try the dizzying feats of the little smoker we had witnessed earlier in the day.

I stared out the bus window at the crowds of people and the freeways packed with cars. We couldn't talk, so I sat in silence. The thoughts came and went in a long daydream. I realized that, in a way, we're all just grains of sand. After 4.5 billion years of Earth and one hundred thousand years of humans, I came out of life's funnel the way I did and landed in my bed, in my house, with my family. The lollygagger landed in his neighborhood, in his house, with his family in inner-city Boston. That's just the way the pile of sand that we call life had collapsed.

Not surprisingly, for a few moments I became obsessed with all the what-ifs of living. As the bus stopped at a yellow traffic light instead of racing through, I wondered how my life might now be completely different. If traffic came to a dead stop for two minutes, I realized it could potentially change my life in drastic ways I'll never even know. I might miss meeting someone great or end up meeting someone horrible because of this two-minute delay.

It only took about seventeen minutes of that what-if kind of thinking to realize that people could drive themselves crazy by doing it too much. It's really not a good way to go through the day. You can what-if yourself right into missing the amazing experiencing of living.

It's at least partially because of sand that today I'm a self-confessed and unapologetic *what-is*-er. I don't tend to care too much for the stories people spin around the what-ifs of situations. People get so distracted by what-ifs that they often overlook what's actually occurring. They live their life atop a big pile of *woulda, coulda, shoulda* that doesn't even exist. They get stuck there and they never let go into the ride of life.

If you think about it (just a little bit), what-if is pretty boring. It's the what-is that makes every day infinitely intriguing. Every person you meet is a living, breathing, absolutely unique what-is standing right in front of you. This is why I'm so fascinated by "the way" of the unique individual. It's breathtaking. Everyone is completely captivating if you are open to seeing it.

Waking up to the perspective of our individual lives being grains of sand does change things. First, you can never see the introduction of the soap opera *Days of Our Lives* without being immediately transported back to the Boston Museum of Science. From time to time, "Like sands through the hourglass, so are the days of our lives" still plays in my head as an adult. I had no idea soap operas were so deep.

More important, how can you ever experience any person, ever again, without realizing what an absolute miracle and a complete happenstance we all are? How can you not look at the good, the bad, and the ugly, and see how it's all a result of an incalculable number of causes and effects coming to bear on a situation? How can you not see how an almost infinite shifting and tilting of grains of sand had to occur for this moment to be experienced exactly the way it is right now?

As I moved on to the miraculous experience of eating my tres leches, my brain accessed another sand incident from my youth. I must have been about five when my town coated the streets of my neighborhood with a gooey type of tar and then covered it with an inch of sand. They did this every few years for reasons I'm sure some civil engineer could explain. All the cars could still drive on the oiled and sanded streets, and within a couple of weeks the street sweeper truck would come pick up all the sand to reveal a road that was both horrible for skateboarding and hurt a lot more when you crashed your bike.

Before the sand was removed, it was very difficult to peddle your bike down the street, but we kids did our level best. One day, a five-year-old version of myself was peddling his bike down the wrong side of his beach of a road. I saw a car coming toward me and became unsure about my navigation skills on the sand. I was worried that the oncoming car was going to hit me.

At the last second I decided I should get to the opposite side of the street. Right before the car was going to pass me, I made a hard right turn. The bike came out from under me, and all I remember was looking up as the entire right side of my body and my bike lay under the car. The driver jumped out of his car to find that I was fine but that the front tire of my bike had been bent beyond being usable.

Now, we could all sit around and think what would have happened had that person been fiddling with the radio dial for just a second instead of watching me. Blah, blah, blah, broken bones, crying, blah, blah, boring! We could go on and on and on speculating, what-if-ing forever, until we were literally bored to death. Let's be honest, a soap opera would be more exciting.

However, what-is-ing is fascinating. So here's the what-is that we know. Because of the accident, I didn't have a bike for a couple weeks, so I had to walk or borrow my sister's bike. One day, she rode me to her friend Robin's house on the back of her bike so I could then walk to my friend Ben's house. Because I was leaving from Robin's house, I went a different route than normal to Ben's house and saw a sign for free puppies. Long story short, that's how I got my dog Stuffin that I loved for sixteen years. It's also how Stuffin bit my friend Peter Figuerido when he was walking past my house. I still think he was taunting my dog and that's why he got bit, but he'll deny it to this day.

What-is-ing my bike accident from a different direction results in the man who almost ran me over putting my bike in the trunk of his car and driving me home. He offered to pay my mother for the bike tire and she refused, but my mom noticed the FOR SALE sign in the back window of his car. We ended up buying the car that almost ran me over.

One year later my mom got in a car accident with that car and needed stitches in her forehead. She stopped at the store on the way home from getting stitches and saw an ad for a Trident gum radio commercial. They wanted real moms to talk in their ad. She applied, and we all got a tremendous kick out of hearing Mom on the radio for the next two or three months. That Trident gum commercial eventually lead to my mom being in a major Hollywood movie, which I'll get to later.

That's what-if-ing versus what-is-ing. I'll take what-is-ing every time.

For me, the funnel of sand led to the simple observation that everything is ultimately rooted in, and results from, a long unbroken chain of cause and effect. When you realize that life is very much like all those grains of sand in a pile, you begin to understand how miraculous life actually is.

On the grand scale, you could consider all the causes and effects that had to come together for this third rock from the sun to come into being. And then consider all the causes and effects that had to come into play over the past 4.5 billion years for us to be here. On a human level, you can think about how sixty thousand years ago Scientific Adam, the father of every human being on this planet, started the chain that led to us sitting here together. How can one not be amazed at all the causes and effects that had to line up back to back in order for us to even exist. That we exist at all—that is the miracle.

Once you see it, *What Is* is everywhere you turn. Battles barely won or lost over thousands of years affected whether our ancestors lived or died—and how they lived if they survived. Three hundred Spartan soldiers saved Greece, and thereby the entirety of Western civilization, by holding off one hundred thousand Persian soldiers in 300 B.C. Over a thousand years later the Persians maintained much of the human advancement of Western culture during the dark ages of Europe. First they almost destroyed it, and then they saved it.

A pile of sand had showed me that everything *is* because of an amazing chain of cause and effect. Each effect becomes the cause for the next effect. We tend to notice the big things that changed the world, but it's also the infinite number of little things that makes us all who we are, all doing what we do. Having the lens of cause and effect on things since you are a child leads to an interesting (and sometimes odd) perspective on things.

However, that's just my wonderfully unique what-is-ing. Your what-is-ing is just as unique, and odd, and wonderful, but so is everyone else's.

A Noble Exchange

Still a nearly extinct carless Californian, after eating my lunch I hopped on my bike to enjoy the glide to Barnes & Noble. It was two miles, downhill all the way. With one side of life always bringing with it the other, I was fully aware that I would be peddling back up this hill to get home. I experienced the excitement of each curb-jumping moment on the way down the hill, just as I certainly would experience my muscles burning as I pedaled up this hill when I returned. To think otherwise would just make non-sense. No matter what was going on, the awareness that life is inevitably a two-sided coin tended to remain with me. One side always brings with it the other.

The good thing about riding my mountain bike in Southern California is that I can ride it on mostly vacant sidewalks. Mountain bikes are built to deal with all types of terrain, so I can jump up and down curbs at will. Thus, I am much less likely to get run over by the drivers chatting on their cell phones.

Pedestrians in Southern California really aren't allowed on the sidewalks unless it's absolutely necessary. It's not an official law or anything, but it is understood that exercise should be done primarily in gymnasiums. The one exception is for those who choose to run or walk on a paved trail of some sort where there are signs pounded into the ground about every fifteen feet saying, KEEP OUR ENVIRONMENT PRISTINE: STAY ON THE TRAIL. Basically, any type of exercise that is not driven to in an automobile is frowned upon. This is why so many of the gymnasiums have valet parking. It all makes sense if you think about it.

After locking up my modest mountain bike with a lock that could survive a direct nuclear strike, I approached the double-doored entrance of Barnes & Noble. As I reached for the door, I noticed a spunky little blonde approaching, briefcase in hand, in fairly traditional business attire. I delayed my entry and let her pass through the doorway unimpeded. I've learned never to expect a tip, but as she passed she gave me a perfectly lovely smile.

"Thank you," she said.

"Anything for a UCLA girl," I quipped.

This comment caused her to plant the business-appropriate one-inch heel of her left shoe into the ground and spin her body, with military precision, exactly one hundred and eighty degrees. Directly facing me, she stared me down with her dominant left eye by turning her head slightly to the right.

"Do I know you?" she asked.

"No, I don't believe so."

She looked down at her clothing and her bag to make sure there were no UCLA stickers or emblems to be seen.

"Then how did you know I went to UCLA?"

"Well," I began, "you're wearing pretty traditional clothing, which is not the most common attire in San Diego, so odds are you work for some large, traditional corporation that requires that you dress that way. Those corporations tend to hire graduates from the major universities."

"Okay, but why UCLA? There are a lot of universities."

"Well, your attire is professional enough for your job, but not quite uptight enough for someone who is actually from the East Coast," I said. "And your body language is too open to be from the East Coast, or the Midwest for that matter. I can tell you didn't grow up dealing with cold weather for months at a time or the Puritan-like undercurrents of those areas. Plus, you walk way too fast to be from the southeastern states. Oh, and the lack of a southern accent helped, too."

"But that just tells you I didn't grow up in those areas. How do you know I didn't go to school there?"

"Your shoulders, neck, and jaw are relaxed in a way you only get with the feeling of being home. You're home, and you like being here. You wouldn't need to get away when you went to college. You're a California girl through and through."

"Oh, my god," she giggled. "Well, there are still a lot of schools in California."

"That's true, but when I opened the door for you, if you went to USC you wouldn't have said thank you. If you went to Berkeley, you wouldn't have said thank you, but you would have also been annoyed. You have too much personality to have gone to UCSD, and your demeanor is too intense, in a good way, to have gone to UC Santa Barbara. And you're not uptight enough to have gone to Stanford. That leaves UCLA."

"Wow, I didn't realize I was that transparent."

"We all are," I confided. "Plus, I guessed. It's not that easy. Now go get your coffee before you're late for your meeting."

I figured I had a fifty-fifty shot, books or coffee. I went with coffee because that's probably what a hardworking, sleep-deprived junior executive would be after. I also took the highly intuitive leap that she had some type of meeting to get to.

"That's unbelievable," she said.

"Just another guess," I said, shrugging my shoulders as we both then turned and went on with our day.

The Barnes & Noble in my town is great. They have big, fluffy chairs that you can sit in and really check out the books that you are considering buying. I also have a soft spot for this particular bookstore because they used to carry my previous book. You've probably not only heard of it, but also actually read it numerous times, so I won't mention the title. Its readership soared into the dozens at one point.

Actually, most people who read the book really enjoyed it because it made them laugh. Thus, all publishing houses banned it because they are secretly run by all those Wall Street insider traders who got caught back in the 1980s. Needless to say, publishing has become a very serious business, with the exception of this book's publisher, who obviously has a tremendous sense of humor.

Anyway, I had a difficult time getting bookstores to carry my self-published rant-in-rhyme because it ignored one of the golden rules of publishing: stay away from the two P's (poetry and pornography). It also made fun of all the books that line the self-improvement aisles of your favorite bookseller. I wound up just shopdropping the book in the local bookstores.

For those of you unfamiliar with the term *shopdrop*, it's a word I made up that means the opposite of *shoplift*. When the right word doesn't exist for something, I have no problem inventing a new one. I would simply smuggle my book into bookstores and in one smooth move place it on their shelves. They're usually looking for the shoplifters, not the shopdroppers, which gave me a big edge. For maximum exposure, I would usually place my book right next to Deepak Chopra. Nice guy, ole' Deepak. He never complained, not even once.

"But how do you make any money if you are *giving* the book-stores your book?" my friends would ask when I told them about my unique shopdrop method of marketing.

"Volume, my friend, volume," I would reply, never pointing out their obvious lack of vision, as that would be rude.

I had glided all the way to my favorite Barnes & Noble in or-der to check out a book called *Einstein and Buddha*, which brings together parallel quotes from quantum physicists and the world of Eastern spiritual thought. For reasons unknown this stuff interests me—always has.

Occasionally some of my childhood friends will try and encour-age me to cut the intellectual stuff and become more like the rabid sports fans that they are. They hope for the day when I will live and die for the New England Patriots and will be willing to stand shirt-less in subzero weather with my body painted red and blue. As far as what-if-ing goes, at least they get me to laugh. In moments of deep mutual respect (or heavy alcohol use), they will often confess that they are just happy I didn't become a Scientologist, cutting checks to the big L. Ron Hubbard in the sky. Of course, when I mention that they might be able to meet John Travolta or Tom Cruise if I converted, they are ready to drive me to the Scientology center themselves.

Somewhere along the line in my life, the cosmic pebble dropped, and I asked the question, *What's the point?* While everything exter-nally appeared to remain exactly as it was before, the experiencing of life was never really the same after that. Once the pebble drops, you can't undo the ripples. They play out the way they do.

I found my way to the science section of the bookstore. On the shelves were the books by Richard Feynman, Stephen Hawking, It-zhak Bentov, Gary Zukav, and others who brought to mind pithy little phrases I had read in their books along the way. It's probably important to note that physicist Bentov's *Jelly Donut Theory of the Universe* is completely unrelated to the Pass the Jelly Principle mentioned earlier in this book. One can't be too careful. I'm already about to be sued by the Scientologists.

I perused the shelves looking for *Einstein and Buddha* but then realized it was just as likely to be shelved in the religion section. When I arrived there I found only a vacant slot where the book would have been. I surmised that it might have been misfiled, so I looked at the books in the general vicinity. No luck.

As I turned to walk away, I spotted *my* copy of the book being held by a redheaded woman sitting to my right. This was not the common Bu-Jew (a Jewish person who's into Buddhism) that frequents such habitats, nor was it even the less populous but also common Hind-Jew (a Jewish person who's into Hinduism). It wasn't even the native waspy intellectual. What sat before me was a spiritually curious Irish Catholic. Whew, talk about self-canceling phrase. They are slightly more common these days than ever before but, like the Himalayan snow leopard, still quite a sight to behold.

By the way, I can spot an Irish Catholic a mile away. It's not just the freckles. It's because I was raised Irish Catholic and can recognize the feisty gene in the bloodline. Also, everyone I knew growing up was either Irish Catholic or Italian. By the way, you never have to say Italian Catholic. It would be like saying *Jewish therapist*. It's redundant. Jesus is *very* big in Italy, kind of like Starbucks in the United States; it's all everybody drinks.

"Excuse me. Is that *Einstein and Buddha* you're holding?" I leaned toward her and asked.

"It certainly is," she gleamed.

Her smile made it clear that she was thrilled to have the book that I wanted in her hot little hands. It was also obvious that she was from a big family. Such delight in possessing something others want can only come from one place: years of exposure to the other side of this equation, where multiple siblings often possessed items she had desired.

"So, are there five or six kids in your family?" I asked.

She paused in a way that indicated slight suspicion, yet intrigue. She then slowly looked me over from head to toe.

"Oh, you're one of those," she challenged.

I was struck by the sophistication of her response. She wanted me spinning in the wind, wondering which one of those "those" I happened to be. Whichever one of "those" that I picked for my-self would be much more accurate than anything an outsider could come up with. It was brilliant, so I ignored it.

"Southie," I said, pointing my index finger directly at her freckled nose.

I was telling her she was from South Boston, not asking her. I knew this because an Irish Catholic from anywhere but the East Coast wouldn't have such a self-contained way about them. An Irish Catholic from New York City would have responded, "Do you mind?" (or a lot worse), in order to be left alone. Only an Irish Catholic from Boston would sit right there and challenge me, but only one from South Boston (Southie) would enjoy it so much. Her accent had been washed away by years of swimming against the Pacific's tide of proper enunciation, but I just knew this was a Southie girl.

"I'm impressed," she smirked. "You must really want this book."

"Actually, quantum physics is a habit I'm trying to kick," I confessed, "but I need a fix, and my sponsor just couldn't talk me down off the ledge this time."

"I don't get it. Do you want it or not?" Southie asked.

"Exactly," I replied, "I couldn't have said it better myself."

"*Exactly* is not an answer."

"But your question sums up the problem," I clarified. "May I share a joke that makes my point?"

"I guess," she acquiesced.

I dove right in:

A small Eastern-block country was taken over in a military coup. As usual, the head general had all the intellectuals gathered up to be executed. In order not to seem mean-spirited, the general granted one final wish to the prisoners on the day before their scheduled execution.

It came time for the country's top two quantum physicists to go before the general and state their final wish. This had to be officially recorded as proof of the new leader's deep humanity and compassion.

"My last wish is that I be allowed to give one concluding lecture on quantum physics to all of my peers," the first physicist said.

"Make it so," the general said, and then turned to the other physicist and asked, "What is your final wish?"

The second quantum physicist replied, "I humbly request that you execute me before my colleague's lecture."

Just as I had begun the joke, Southie's friend arrived on the scene. She was a tall brunette with bee sting lips and a set of bolt-on fake boobs that appeared freshly polished from the low-cut blouse she was wearing. I appreciated that she brought them out to share with everyone. It's that spirit of giving that makes the world a better place. I'm more of an *au naturel* kind of guy, but still, the effort on her part did not go unnoticed.

Southie's friend appeared to be one type of the standard Southern California Woman who rolls off the assembly line on a regular basis. This model was also available in redhead and blonde, with an optional lower back tattoo, depending on the level of midlife crisis and relationship status.

Her clarity on the issue of sexual attraction was refreshing. She wasn't going half way like some of the dilettantes out there. She was going straight to the source—the visually stimulated male brain. She didn't choose what the primal parts of men's brains found attractive, but she'd be damned if some other woman was going to win the game while she sat on the bench.

She was just "passing the jelly" like each and every one of us, just doing what we do because that's what we do. She was like all of us out there finding our own *way* in order to survive, get by, and sometimes to thrive. Ours *ways* are unique, but no more than anyone else. She was keeping herself in the game of physical attraction for as long as she could, the best way she knew how. She was no different than the much-adored aging athlete doing their best to stay in the game they love.

I wasn't expecting much conversation from The Gamer. That had been my experience with this model in the past. I had her all labeled and categorized in my brain. She was neatly tucked away in the *one-of-those* files. I was about to find out that I was totally wrong.

"That's a horrible joke," The Gamer said with a tone of clear annoyance and a lack of facial expression that was intriguing.

Yow! She's hardboiled, I thought to myself. Then I strapped in for a bumpy ride.

"My sense of humor is an acquired taste for some," I asserted.

"Like Rocky Mountain Oysters?" she barbed back.

I was struck by how totally wrong I was about The Gamer. Her wit was as sharp as the Botox needles that had been stuck in her forehead. It was a pleasant surprise.

"My point is that we mostly live in a world where the cause and effect laws of Newton govern our everyday lives, not the esoteric but also true, laws of quantum physics. When you are about to be executed, quantum physics might help you with the idea of dying, but it won't help you with the reality of being executed."

"I believe we create our own reality every day," The Gamer injected. "Quantum physics proves it."

I could understand why The Gamer would believe we create our own reality. I'm sure there was at least one plastic surgeon that would attest to the physical realities The Gamer had created through the application of money to the surgeon's bank account. But saying that the world can be changed by the actions we take is not the same as saying we can create our own reality. Otherwise, I'm pretty sure a few billion people on the planet would wish away their current life circumstances.

"Interesting," I said with a nod of genuine appreciation. "I'm attracted to the idea that everything has already happened, so all we do is wake up every day to find out what we already did. Quantum physics proves that too."

"Everything has already happened," Southie repeated. "I like that."

"It's a nice place to be, isn't it?" I said directly to Southie. "Kinda takes the pressure off, especially when you're the type of person who is already doing the best you can anyway."

"That's ridiculous," The Gamer challenged. "Where did you get that theory?"

"Well, for one, do you know who Stephen Hawking is?"

"Yeah, he's one of the world's great physicists," The Gamer spat with a palpable annoyance.

Gamer, you're as tough as a coffin nail, I thought to myself. *I do love chatting with you.* But I noticed that my eyes kept being drawn to her puffy lips, so I was consciously trying to avoid any full-of-lip-type comments or phrases about stirring up hornets' nests. I didn't want The Gamer to walk away.

"Hawking wrote, 'ultimately, everything is pre-determined, but we don't know what's going to happen anyway, so what's the difference?'" I said with a pleasant chuckle that implied, *Hey, we're all in this together, so let's play nice.*

Southie was with me, but The Gamer would have none of it.

"So what's your point?" The Gamer snapped, glaring at me like we were trapped in an airtight space, and I was breathing her last bit of oxygen.

"Quantum physics is great stuff, but we live in a Newtonian world," I began. "What happens right now is determined by the massive inertia of a long chain of cause and effect that started at the beginning of time and continues today."

I needed a good example to make my point. I wanted something Southie, at least, could relate to. It had to be well grounded in her life experience, but it also had to get to the root of what I was pointing toward. Then I realized that Southie's culinary experience growing up was probably similar to mine. Her ethnicity and geographical origin predicted that a baked potato was on her dinner plate every night as a child, so I went with it.

"Just think about all that had to happen for me and my friend from Southie here to be standing in this store having this conversation," I said looking at The Gamer and resting my hand on Southie's shoulder. "We could examine the chain of cause and effect anywhere from the Big Bang to this morning, but I could give you an example that starts in the year 1531, if you're interested."

"Fifteen thirty-one?" The Gamer scoffed.

Her skepticism was displayed not only by her tone of voice, but with the supporting eye roll you get from tilting your forehead down as you look directly at someone. I think the Botox injections probably prevented her from being able to raise her eyebrows, so this was her only physical way to project sarcasm.

"Oh, yes, 1531 is a very important year for the eventual meeting of Southie and me," I said, purposely using "Southie" as her name to see if she would object. (Let the record show: she did not object.)

"I'm sure she is very well acquainted with the object of which I am about to speak," I said to The Gamer, "because 1531 was the year Pizarro discovered the potato in Peru."

"The potato?" The Gamer snarled.

"I love potatoes. I grew up on potatoes," Southie confirmed.

"Yes, the lowly potato. Europe didn't have the potato until Pizarro brought it back from South America. By 1650 the potato had reached Ireland where it became the staple crop of the Irish. As we all know, the Brits had only one problem with Ireland: it had too many Irish. But with the potato, which produced four times as many calories per acre as grains, an Irish family of four could survive with just one acre of land and one cow. The Irish were very hard to get rid of because they made such a cheap source of slavery—I mean labor—for their British landlords. Thus, our distant ancestors survived because of the lowly potato."

"Is there a point to this?" The Gamer asked.

Southie, by the way, was transfixed by my every word (justifying again my bias toward redheads).

"I'll make it quick," I continued. "So the potato saves the Irish, but then the potato famine hits in the 1840s. The Irish are dying in massive numbers, so millions leave Ireland and go to the U.S. and other parts of the world. Many land in New England, and this attracts other Irish who came later, like my grandparents. Southie's parents or grandparents arrived in Boston somewhere within that chain of cause and effect. Bing, bang, bong, each of our parents meet in New England, have kids—cause and effect—cause and effect—and we end up in this bookstore talking. But none of it would have happened if not for the potato. Without the potato, Southie and I probably wouldn't even exist."

"Was that clear?" I inquired.

"Some physicists say that if you really truly believed that you could walk on water, then you really could," said The Gamer.

Her complete disregard for my enthralling history of the potato did not go unnoticed. It didn't seem like she was being intentionally hostile. Her words just came out that way.

"That all *sounds* great," I explained, "but show me just one person who can actually do it, now, today, anywhere in the world, and I'll gladly throw out everything I've said. I want to believe in magic too, but when it comes down to it, we live in a pretty dense Newtonian world."

The Gamer didn't respond, but I was about to make a very important point, so I turned and faced her directly.

"It's already a miracle that we are walking around on land; why do you need someone to walk on water?"

No response, again.

"When you were little, did you ever play 'I'll show you mine, if you show me yours?'" I asked.

"Excuse me?" The Gamer snarled.

My attempt at humor had gotten her flustered, which surprised me, but at least she was back in the conversation.

"Look," I said as I reached over and grabbed a small hardcover book off the shelf. "Sir Isaac Newton and I predict that this book will drop to the floor when I let it go. Let's all watch." I let the book go and it landed flat on the floor. "Fascinating," I said, "An actual demonstration of a theory. Not that difficult, really. Watch, I'll do it again." I bent over and picked up the book and then held it out in front of me. I let it go, and again it fell to the floor. "Look, it did it again. A repeatable demonstration of a theory; now that's not really asking too much, is it? Shall we head over to the local pool to see a person, any person, walk on water? What do you think?"

"So you have some big secret that all these books are missing?" The Gamer said, pointing at the bookshelves.

"The real secret is—you are going to die," I replied. "Your quantum particles may live on forever, but you are going to die."

I let my dense Newtonian words sit out there in the silence, so The Gamer and Southie could experience their weight.

"Now that you know the secret," I whispered, "the question is—how are you going to live?"

"We live in a Newtonian world," I continued. "All your quantum particles are packed into a Newtonian body that is going to die. That home you live in was built using good old Newtonian physics, as was the car you drive every day. And your car might be made of quantum particles, but you had better get out of the way if its Newtonian-built bumper if it's driving toward you."

"So what exactly are you saying?" asked The Gamer, appearing almost interested.

"I'm pointing out that Einstein's theories really apply only at the extremely minute and extremely massive ends of the spectrum. Life is a Newton Sandwich, with only the thinnest layer of Einstein bread on each side."

"So you don't think we create our own reality?" Gamer asked.

I really like her, I thought to myself as The Gamer's words came forth. Sure, it was a she-doesn't-like-me-at-all, unrequited kind of liking, but that's not the worst thing in the world. Besides, a long-term relationship with The Gamer would never work out.

"No, I think our cause-and-effect world creates us." I turned to Southie and said, "You never answered my question—was it five or six kids in your family?"

"Six," Southie replied.

"And you're the fourth or the fifth child," I stated.

"I was the fourth," she offered, slapping my upper arm.

Don't be confused by the slap. The rules from fourth grade still apply to adults. When a woman voluntarily touches you, it's a good thing. It means she likes you.

"How'd you know that?" Southie asked.

"It's just our cause-and-effect world. You're not serious enough to be the oldest, and not submissive enough to be the second child who grew up under the thumb of the oldest. And you're not carefree enough to be the youngest child. Oh, and you're not angry enough to be the third child who got lost in the crowd along the way. That only leaves number four or five." I said.

"You're a freak," she said, but I'm pretty sure she meant it in a good way.

"That's just cause and effect, my friend," I responded. "It's a Newtonian world—we're just living in it." After a pause I added with a smirk, "Some of us are just more into it than others."

"Yeah, I was right. You are one of *those*," Southie replied.

Her tone implied that her statement was negative, but the accompanying bright eyes and smile confirmed that the opposite was true. I was free once again to define her word *those* in any way I chose. I appreciated Southie's style, but at the moment, I just didn't have time to pick out a label for myself (plus, my labels change all the time; it's hard to keep up).

"And the fact that you are so comfortable with me probably means you had a lot of brothers. I'll guess, what, four?" I inquired.

"That's right," she said, laughing.

"And your friend here had no brothers," I stated with a gentle wave of my hand toward The Gamer. I was in the zone, so naturally, I decided to push my luck. "But maybe one younger sister. My brotherly way of being isn't that familiar to her, but she grew up used to being in a position of dominance over someone younger than she was, so she's not an only child."

"That's pretty good," Southie said to The Gamer in partial confirmation of my guesses (and they were guesses) as The Gamer remained silent.

"See, the Newtonian world can be just as fascinating as the trendy universe of quantum physics. We all come in with the genes our parents gave us. Added to that is the conditioning we received as a child. We then pile on the rest of our life conditioning, and that's the lens that filters each life situation we encounter and react to. It's all our genes and conditioning; it's all cause and effect. It's incredible if you think about it."

We all stood in silence for what seemed like a very long time, but was really about three seconds.

"It's because of our genes and conditioning," I continued, "that we wake up each morning basically the same person as we were the day before. Without even trying, I might add. That's why your friends are your friends—because their conditioned behavior is within a range that you generally like. For instance, I've always liked you Southie girls, so I'm glad cause and effect brought us both here today."

"Oh, *please*," The Gamer groaned.

"See," I said to Southie, "you don't seem too surprised by your friend's interaction with me because it's probably a somewhat normal way for her to be. 'It's just the way she is,' as we say."

"That's true," Southie said as she glanced at The Gamer.

"Everyone is pretty much doing the best they can as they go through life," I continued. "They are the culmination of a very long chain of cause and effect with a massive amount of inertia behind it. That's why it can be so difficult for people to change. And that's why I often say, 'Everybody is doing the best they can.'"

"Do you go around doing this to everybody?" Southie asked, grinning.

"Not really. Just the women who are holding the book I want."

"Oh, so you're a player," The Gamer said with an unexpected smile.

"No, I have no desire to manipulate you for my own gain. I just enjoyed chatting with you two," I said, as I began walking away. "It was nice meeting both of you."

"Bye," said Southie as The Gamer looked on blankly.

I think The Gamer understood that, like everyone else, I was just doing the best I can. But maybe not. Although we are all completely unique, The Gamer was put together in such a way that our gears didn't really mesh, but they *almost* meshed. It was like having a metric wrench that was close to working on an American bolt, but wasn't quite close enough. That's why I found her so delightful. I'd think I had a good grip on her, but as soon as I tried to engage her, my grip would slip away. I had no idea what she was going to do next, which I guess is true with everyone. But with her, it was just so obvious that I appreciated her reminding me of that basic truth.

That's What You Get

I meandered away from Southie and The Gamer and wondered what had caused me to be constantly fascinated with our world of cause and effect. Life's long chain of connected events seemed so mundane to most other people that it went virtually unnoticed. I wandered by the children's section and saw all the little kids poring over their books. I remembered sitting on my mom's lap when I was a child and reading *Curious George* over and over again. I wondered if it was my love of Curious George and his friend, the man with the yellow hat, who helped make me the way I am. Or maybe I liked Curious George so much because I was already that way: curious.

Then I was struck by the fact that from an early age I was getting rather dramatic lessons in cause and effect, not just from Curious George, but also from the world around me. I stood in place and began laughing as I recalled my favorite and most vivid childhood memory. My mind had shot me back to kindergarten, just like it was yesterday.

I'm sure my kindergarten class of 1970 was much like the many classes that came before it. Like all kindergartens, the intention was to break the spirit of small children. This was done to create obedient members of society who would be ready for elementary school, so most parents lent their blind support to the program.

Our Lady of Grace was the perfect setting for molding children. The main building of the school was connected directly to the church. To five-year-olds, this meant that Jesus was always watching. Plus, there were statues and pictures of virgin mothers, saints, popes, and bishops everywhere you turned. The message was clear: kindergarteners are at the bottom of the Catholic totem pole, so behave.

Sister Mary Darerca was our teacher, and the first lesson for our class was to master the recitation of her full name, in unison and on cue. The first day's endless chorus of little voices saying, "Yes, Sister Mary Darerca," "No, Sister Mary Darerca," "Never, Sister Mary Darerca," "Always, Sister Mary Darerca," and "Thank you, Sister Mary Darerca," allowed her name to roll off our tongues as well as if she had taken the saint name "Bob." Her enthusiasm regarding her *nom de nun* was just another reminder that a two-named nun was always a sign of double trouble for young Catholic boys. Such nuns appeared blessed with a more ambitious piety than the slacker nuns who had chosen only one saint's name.

Our teacher had taken the stock "Mary" for her first name (after the Virgin Mother), which had all the flavor of a communion wafer. But "Darerca" was an interesting second choice. St. Darerca was a fifth century Irish woman who had given birth to fifteen sons, ten of whom had become bishops. Our teacher apparently nurtured the hope that her classroom labors could birth a future bishop or two from the small flock of children she lectured to each day. But she never flaunted her optimism in front of the students, which we all appreciated.

She seemed nice enough for a nun. Her uniform consisted of the typical black and white headgear sported by nuns, a long-sleeved white shirt, and a gray skirt. This was much less intimidating for small children than the penguin suit worn by other nuns. She was what some would call a handsome woman, solid and stocky, but not fat. Her wimple hid all of her hair, which made age determination problematic, but she was probably rapidly approaching her thirtieth year.

When Sister Mary Darerca greeted the parents and children each morning, you could tell that she really did want to be warm and cheerful. Her wanting it so much made her *almost* warm and cheerful, but not quite. When she smiled, she almost smiled, but not quite. Her smile never reached her eyes. That's how we all know a real smile from a fake one—even if you don't consciously know it, you know it. If it doesn't make the corners of the eyes crinkle a bit, then you are only trying to smile.

Sister Mary Darerca was well intentioned in her almostness, but her solid build and nervous energy made her a stress-filled cross between Mother Teresa and Lou Costello. Imagining such a "love child" may be difficult for you, so just try putting a nun's habit on Lou Costello; that will cover most of it. For those of you who are advanced, picture Lou in a nun's habit while he does the famous Abbott and Costello *Who's on First* routine. It gives the routine a whole new twist and helps you realize what we five-year-olds were up against.

Let's just say that Sister Mary Darerca was devoted to her faith and had the best of intentions, but she was a bit too high strung to enjoy it. For her, life was a wrestling match. She was engaged in the constant battle of wrestling life to the ground and pinning it to the mat until it submitted. Since that seemed to also be the goal of kindergarten, one would think they were a perfect match.

What made Sister Mary Darerca odd is that she also yearned to fly. She was that baby bird perched on the edge of a treetop nest, too anxious to jump out of the nest on her own. She needed someone to give her a good shove, so all her potential could be realized. My friend Pinky was just the kid for the job.

Pinky and I were well into our second week of school, and all seemed to be going well. Sister Mary Darerca had established a finely tuned and rigid routine. We knew when recess was. We knew when snack time was. We knew when nap time was. In between those times, we did schoolwork. It seemed pretty clear to Sister Mary Darerca, but there was a lot of gray area in that schedule if you think about it, especially for my friend Pinky.

Pinky's real name was Jim. One year earlier he had worn his sister's pink Snoopy sweatshirt out to play, and some of the older kids called him Pinky. The nickname stuck for the next fourteen years until he went off to college, where it was consciously and effectively shunned into near extinction. Even when I try to call him Jim as an adult, I'll often slip and refer to him as Pink. He doesn't seem to mind, as long as the rest of the world knows him as Jim.

As a five year old, Pink was a freckled, redheaded ball of energy. He was also a kind-hearted kid who didn't seem to have a mean-spirited bone in his entire body. This is why Pink's actions on this day of which I'm about to speak were a true testament to the human spirit. He sacrificed himself for others and became the hero that we all long for, but never really expect.

Our individual desks at Our Lady of Grace numbered twenty-five. They were configured in a U-shape with the open end facing the chalkboard. Pinky and I both sat at desks with our backs to a wall of windows. At one end of the windows was Sister Mary Darerca's desk; at the other were all of our personal toys brought from home.

On a day that will live on in infamy, Pinky and I finished our class work early. We saw no reason why the slow pace of the other students should inhibit our desire to entertain ourselves, so Pinky walked over to the window and retrieved his fully loaded G.I. Joe Jeep. Sister Mary Darerca didn't seem to notice as Pinky returned to his desk with jeep in hand.

We both pulled out our chairs so that the three students between us would not hamper the path of our play. Without speaking, we began pushing the jeep back and forth to each other. In retrospect, it may have been a bit noisy on the tiled floor of the classroom, but that really wasn't our fault now, was it?

I'm pretty sure that kindergarten rules specified no talking, which Pink and I were obeying to the letter. As far as we could tell, everything was as kosher as could be in our little Catholic schoolroom. We pushed the truck back and forth to each other, enjoying the current state of kindergarten harmony. On the fifth launch from Pinky toward me, Sister Mary Darerca appeared between us and quite rudely intercepted the speeding truck in her nervous little hands.

Pinky and I had both been taught good manners, but apparently Pinky was more of a stickler for etiquette than I. He found it intolerable that someone would just take his toy without a "May I?" "Please," or "Thank you." Frankly, my five-year-old self could understand his initial dismay. The blame was obviously hers. Pinky and I were both clear on the rules and regulations, and there was nothing that specifically restricted the rolling of jeeps back and forth when all your schoolwork was done. Nothing.

I sat there like a little child who had just had his toy taken away, which I was, but Pinky became a real-life freedom fighter. The tyranny we had been suffering under for two straight weeks had finally produced a rebel willing to inspire others. Pinky instinctively knew the Germans had created kindergarten, so some type of blitzkrieg response would have immediately crushed any organized revolt.

Hours of G.I. Joe playtime had apparently made Pinky an astute military tactician. This is most likely why he chose to employ guerilla tactics. They were both bold and unexpected in this kindergarten setting, but even he could not have expected to achieve the success he did on this day.

"That's my jeep. Gimme my jeep," Pinky commanded as he leapt from his seat.

"Sit down, James," Sister Mary Darerca ordered.

We could all sense that Sister Mary Darerca's dismissive tone meant only more trouble for her. After all, Pinky's main objection was her lack of common courtesy. The jeep was basically being held hostage, and hostage taking of any kind cannot be tolerated by freedom fighters. Sister Mary Darerca stood firmly with the jeep in both hands, resting it against her belly. This is when things got interesting.

"Gimme my jeep!" Pinky screamed while his hands shot toward his toy with the lightning speed of a five-year old ninja.

Sister Mary Darerca spun sideways with a surprising grace and quickness. She protected the jeep and allowed his attack to glide past her as she walked toward her desk. It was now clear that this would be no ordinary battle.

Pinky's commitment to the cause was extraordinary. A five-year-old taking on the entire kindergarten system is not an everyday event. He continued to jump toward his toy as Sister Mary Darerca bobbed and weaved her way toward her desk. You could tell she was wondering what had caused things to go so terribly wrong. Pinky was about to decode her defensive strategy when she wisely decided to hold the jeep above her head.

"Gimme my jeep. Gimme my jeep!" was Pinky's mantra.

His cries had galvanized the masses of little people, and we all began to laugh and celebrate the spirit of our new leader. Pinky's attempts to retrieve his toy were currently failing due to his height. He remedied this by standing on Sister Mary Darerca's desk chair and then turned to feel the wave of admiration that was flowing toward him from his fellow students.

"Gimme my jeep!" he cried, leaping skyward toward his toy.

Sister Mary Darerca spun clockwise like a silent prima ballerina wearing a habit and holding a jeep above her head. The maneuver made Pinky miss completely both the jeep and Sister Mary Darerca, which caused him to hesitate. She took the opportunity to outflank him by positioning herself in front of her desk and, most important, away from her chair.

By the time Pinky recovered, the cheering hoards were completely behind his cause. Some were clapping; some were screaming. We were all thrilled that the inmates were now running the asylum. With such galvanized supporters, Pinky was about to take the engagement to a level that had never before been seen in kindergarten classroom history.

In a complex series of maneuvers that I can still see as if it happened yesterday, Pinky climbed onto Sister Mary Darerca's desk chair and then stepped onto the middle of her desk. He paused and assessed the magnitude of the situation. In a moment of true inspiration, Pinky cocked his little carrot-topped head back, pounded his fists on his chest and, at the top of his lungs, did his very best Tarzan imitation.

"Ahhhhhh, ahhh, AHHHHH!" he bellowed and then began running across the top of his teacher's desk toward his jeep.

Sister Mary Darerca recognized that the Tarzan imitation and the projectile redhead coming toward her were definite *signs*. It wasn't the Biblical raining of frogs or locusts, but it was pretty close. She had lost control of the situation.

The crowd was going absolutely wild. Our carrot-topped super-hero's commitment was undeniable. He was about to launch himself into midair and potentially go down in flames like the Hindenburg. Some five-year-old version of "Oh, the humanity" could be seen on all the students' faces as the moment of truth arrived.

With every bit of effort his freckled little self could muster, Pinky hurled himself toward Sister Mary Darerca and his jeep. Whirling Dervish Darerca outmaneuvered him again with a dip-bend-spin move that caused Pinky to entirely miss his precious toy. He was fly-ing through the air, about to crash onto the tiled floor, when Sister Mary Darerca continued her spin so that Pinky landed on and slid down her back. The two of them had become a finely tuned Martha Graham dance company, defying both gravity and the normal awk-wardness of their bodies within it.

Like any true artist, Pinky sensed that the performance had not only peaked but was rapidly coming to an end. He arched his low back and pumped his chest out as he stood facing the crowd. His right arm straightened as he raised it toward the ceiling with the palm of his hand skyward. He then flopped forward, completing a dramatic bow. It was similar to the Bugs-Bunny-plays-a-conductor bow we had seen on TV just the week before, but I'm sure that's only a coincidence. His adoring fans roared in appreciation.

Pinky rose from his bow and spread his arms toward the crowd in a gesture of thanks. Sister Mary Darerca grabbed Pinky's right arm with her left hand. The newly born Sister of Spin then took all of Pinky's ef-forts to escape and redirected them. Like an Aikido master at a square dance, she guided Pinky into a perfectly executed do-si-do. They had become spiraling partners in a kindergarten dance. The crowd couldn't have been any more impressed with the performance.

"Principal's office," she said in a relieved but exhilarated tone as she escorted Pinky out of the room.

As Sister Mary Darerca and Pinky left, the crowd sat in stunned silence. I think it is safe to say that this was as close to a religious experience as we were going to get at Our Lady of Grace, and we had Pinky to thank for it.

When Sister Mary Darerca returned, something about her had changed. She had been transformed from a wrestler into a ballerina. There was pep in her normally rigid step, and her face appeared genuinely relaxed. It seems Pinky caused her to stretch herself beyond her normal limits and she realized everything was still okay. We could all see she had gone from a shaking baby bird to a graceful, gliding adult on the updraft of a victorious encounter with life. I'm sure she noticed how calm we all were as well. When she sent us off at the end of the day, she did so with a real smile, crinkled eyes and all. I'm pretty sure she had Pinky to thank for that.

When I got home from kindergarten that day, I walked three houses down to Pinky's and knocked on the door. "Can Pinky come out and play?" I asked.

"No, Pinky won't be able to come out and play for the rest of the week," Pink's mom declared.

I was genuinely confused with her response. I could think of no good reason why I shouldn't be able to play with my friend.

"Why?" I asked.

"Because that's what you get when you act up in school," she said.

Apparently, Pinky's mom had been called by the principal's office and was asked to take her son home. When she entered the building and passed the school janitor, he took it upon himself to give her an assessment of her child. After all, his job had allowed him to spend years surrounded by children of all ages.

"That's one crazy kid you got there, lady," he said.

It was clear that she appreciated his deep psychological insight, as years later she was still unable to chuckle about the comment.

Pinky's fight for the cause of all kindergarteners around the world had not only gotten him grounded at home, but it had also gotten him court-martialed at school. He was suspended from our fair Lady of Grace for the rest of the week. He did return the next week with no further incidents, so I guess "that's what you get" really works when it's done right.

The Pinky Revolt still ranks as one of my most inspirational childhood memories, but the life of a freedom fighter is not all glory. Kindergarten eventually beat Pinky down, broke his spirit, and made him a functional member of society because "that's what you get," eventually, from kindergarten.

It was another couple of years before I remember hearing the words "that's what you get," but then I began hearing them all the time. It all started up again when my best friend, Ben, and I could be seen carrying tackle boxes and fishing poles along the wooded paths of the East Providence reservoir. To the casual observer, we were two seven-year-old boys going fishing. In actuality, it was a covert, Big Foot search-and-discovery expedition. The binoculars around my neck were the clue.

Although there had never been an actual sighting of Big Foot in New England, there were plenty of places for him to go unnoticed. Apart from our local reservoir, there was the abandoned granite quarry known as The Pit. Long before I was born, water had filled The Pit, and it was now a place of legend. Supposedly bodies had been dumped there and would never be found because the water was 350 feet deep. Obviously, if you were Big Foot, The Pit would be a very likely choice of residence.

It was summertime, so Ben and I would go fishing every couple of days at some of his favorite locations. There was Perch Peak, Catfish Cove, and my all-time favorite, Sun Fish Spot. Ben was never afraid to stretch a bit for an alliteration, which I've always appreciated about him. However, his fishing locations had more to do with his desire for a cool-sounding name than any actual fish residing in the water there. Thus, I know from experience the truth of the statement, "The worse the fisherman, the better the philosopher."

On lucky days, Ben's Uncle Bob would let us use his rowboat that was otherwise chained to a tree at the reservoir's wooded edge. Ben and I were both too small to individually row the boat very well, but Uncle Bob showed us that we were also small enough to both fit on the main seat. This allowed us to each hold one oar. If we rowed together, we could get around pretty well. With no life jackets to slow us down, it was easy going.

"Stay away from the falls," Uncle Bob would call out as we headed off.

This was good advice, as the waterfall was at least a ten-foot drop and could ruin Uncle Bob's boat.

Our fishing mostly involved the standard floats, fishing hooks, and worms that we had dug up in a nearby field. Borrowing some deep-sea fishing lures from Ben's dad was also an occasional occurrence. There were some days when we could no longer be satisfied with sunfish, catfish, and perch. We were going for the big catch, maybe a marlin, or some giant tuna. We'd even occasionally go with an eel lure, hoping that some moray eel may have migrated up from Florida for the summer. We were optimists—what can I say?

Ben's dad gently encouraged us to use our regular fishing gear, which might have resulted in actually catching fish, but he never forced the issue.

"Don't lose my lures," was his only order when we were leaving. "Did you catch anything?" was his only question when we returned. "Well, that's what you get," was his repeated wisdom when we caught not a single fish.

For some reason, "Well, that's what you get" seemed to be one of the main methods of teaching in my neighborhood. It was a simple recognition of actions and consequences, the simple acknowledgement of our cause-and-effect world. Ben and I did finally learn that it didn't matter if we were at Rough Rock Ridge or Bass Bay. Our deep-sea lures weren't going to do much good in our local reservoir.

In the years since, I've also learned that searching for Big Foot in the woods of the local reservoir or at The Pit was some of the most fun I've ever had. The fun was in the adventure, not in the actual sighting of a New England yeti, so sometimes "that's what you get" also means you had a great time.

This simple recognition of actions and consequences led to my experiencing some reasonably effective parenting techniques. When I was eight, my brother, sister, and I took a trip to the local Kmart. While in the store, my sister and I ripped open a bag of balloons and took some samples home for testing purposes. After all, purchasing a whole bag of balloons was a big commitment with my limited annual income of birthday and Christmas money.

On the car ride home, my little brother was in the front passenger seat of the car. My sister and I were in the back. The front passenger seat is the least safe place to put a small child, but my brother had called it first when we stepped outside the doors of the store. He had earned the rights to his seat, and we weren't about to bend the rules for some abstract safety statistics.

With my brother enjoying all that comes with sitting in the front seat of the car, my sister and I couldn't resist checking out our booty from the big caper. We pulled the balloons out of our pockets and laid them on the seat between us. As we reveled in our newfound riches, the lesson that nothing was free was about to be branded into my life experience.

Kmart was only three miles from our home and seatbelts were only for long trips, so little brother Bill was not strapped in. When he unexpectedly stood up and turned around, the jig was up. In a fraction of a second he recognized that a major heist had taken place.

"Dad, Dad! They stole balloons from Kmart! They stole balloons from Kmart!" he hollered.

My dad glanced back to see the balloons on the seat. In an instant he was spinning the wheel with the palm of his hand and making a U-turn. The centrifugal force pushed all children against the passenger-side doors. My father performed the right arm reach of protection for my little brother in the front seat, but my sister and I were sardined in the backseat. After his U-turn was complete, my father turned and looked at the two felons in the backseat.

"Let's see what you get when you steal," he said.

The dizzying high of thieves at the end of a successful job came crashing down under the weight of impending negative consequences. In moments we were back at Kmart about to confront our fate as my father headed into the manager's office.

"Let me see what I can do," were the words my dad left us with.

His tone and facial expression made clear that he might not be able to alter the consequences that come from stealing. It's pretty safe to say that my sister and I were terrified. Even my little brother was feeling bad for being a snitch, which means things must have been pretty tense. After all, ratting on his older siblings was one of his main pleasures, since he so often got the short end of the sibling stick.

I had the added stress of having seen a few scenes of *Cool Hand Luke* a couple of months earlier. My father had called me into the living room to see the part where Paul Newman eats fifty hardboiled eggs. Unfortunately, my mind was currently on the chain gang scenes. Men working with pick axes and shovels on a dusty road in the heat of summer were the visions in my head. Thoughts of having to say "yes, boss" to the prison guards all the time were not very appealing either.

"Let's go," my dad said as he waved us into the office, "it's up to the manager now."

"Show him what you took," my Dad ordered as we stood in front of the manager's desk.

My sister and I pulled the balloons from our pockets as projectile tears shot out of our eyes. Our shaking little balloon-holding hands and our watery eyes were genuine as the store manager decided our fate. I have no doubt my dad was standing behind us nodding at him to give it to us good. Fortunately, the manager took pity on us.

"Well, I don't think we'll call the police this time," he warned, "but if you ever steal from a store again, that's what you'll get."

As far as life lessons go, this was a pretty good one. "That's what you'll get" were the words used to describe the concept that actions have consequences. I was so traumatized that I never even thought of shoplifting ever again. Of course, shopdropping is an entirely different issue.

After the failed Kmart heist, I came to realize "that's what you get" was actually a very common phrase in the everyday happenings of my neighborhood. This was primarily because I was surrounded by cutting-edge social scientists regularly doing experiments on human nature, cause and effect, and so on.

You see, drivers during rush hours would often attempt to cut 3.7 seconds off their commute by cutting through my neighborhood. The problem was that my neighborhood consisted of mostly Irish Catholic families. Our understanding of the need for diversity meant there were also a few Italian families allowed as well, but this still meant that everyone was brainwashed—uh, I mean, everybody had a divine faith that using any type of birth control would lead to eternal damnation. The result was that my little neighborhood was jam packed with kids. My grade at the local elementary school had thirty-five kids just from my neighborhood.

Many of the short-cutters would drive much too fast for a neighborhood brimming with children. At any given time, there were simultaneous games of street hockey, dodge ball, hop scotch, kick the can, and jump rope being played on the streets and in the yards. Fathers would often yell at a passing car to slow down. Naturally, the kids would seize the opportunity to scream at the speeding cars too. A chance to scream at an adult without threat of punishment was not to be missed. A driver would often get multiple "Slow downs!" screamed at him from kids of all ages, heights, and tones of voice as he drove by, but none of this seemed to have an effect.

One day a frequent commuter, who seemed to be increasing his speed by the week, almost ran over one of the neighborhood kids. It was a heart-pounding, jaw-clenching screeching of tires that stopped literally inches from my little cousin Colleen. She was unharmed, but the problem of cars speeding down our streets needed to be dealt with.

Colleen's father was my Uncle Jimmy. He was the neighborhood's notorious problem solver. Every neighborhood had one in those days, and he was ours. If there was an elderly person who needed their trees trimmed, he was there. If someone's car was stuck after a snowstorm, Uncle Jimmy was the man on the job. He was the one who pressed the city to put up stop signs to slow down the commuters. He was also the one whose daughter was almost killed, so we were all pretty sure he'd be the one to solve the problem, at least with this particular speeder.

The next week when the same car came speeding down our street at its regular time, the driver found himself being blocked by an older group of kids playing street hockey. I'm pretty sure the exchange between the driver and my Uncle Jimmy started out as one of words, but in short order my uncle was pulling the guy out of the car through the driver's side window. In the end, the speeder wasn't physically harmed, but he was definitely emotionally shaken.

Even as a small child, I knew there was something significant about the response from people in the neighborhood. "Well, that's what you get" was the phrase I kept hearing. It wasn't said in a mean or a happy way. It was just a matter-of-fact, common sense tone that recognized the *what is* nature of life.

That night my Uncle Jimmy was arrested by the local police for pulling an innocent commuter out the window of his car.

"Well, that's what you get," said in that same matter-of-fact tone, were the words heard throughout the neighborhood. Folks were simply acknowledging the law of cause and effect. Actions and consequences were just playing themselves out. Eventually, even the driver came to realize that he bore some responsibility for what took place between he and my uncle. He had a change of heart and dropped his legal charges.

Coincidentally, a few days before the charges were dropped, my Uncle Jimmy had followed his speeding nemesis to his place of employment and smashed in every window and light in his car with a baseball bat. I'm pretty sure you can guess how the people in my neighborhood responded when they heard the news. "Well, that's what you get" echoed through the streets.

We'll never really know what influenced the speeder's decision to drop the charges because we never saw him again. With communication skills like Uncle Jimmy's, that's also what you get: people just stop coming around.

Even as a little kid I began to understand that in life there are merely actions and consequences; it's not really personal. It's people doing what they do, and there are positive and negative outcomes from their interactions. It's all as natural as snow falling on a mountaintop. Most of the time the sun gently melts it away and it becomes the water we drink, but sometimes forces come together and there's an avalanche. I guess that's what makes people doing what they do so fascinating. Uncle Jimmy's approach was certainly not what Gandhi would have done, but then again, Gandhi didn't live in my neighborhood.

Shortly after Uncle Jimmy's example of aggressive problem solving, the older kids in the neighborhood took on a more passive-aggressive approach to dealing with the speeders. It was much more fun and had far fewer legal costs associated with it. Thus, the game "Hubcap" had a very short but eventful life during the winter of 1973.

The game of Hubcap took place only at the corner of Rye and Scott streets and required a minimum of two players. The rest of the game was based on simple physics. When a speeding car approached the intersection's stop sign, its tires would run over the ever-present potholes. The impact was enough that it could potentially jar loose a car's hubcap. This basic understanding was the foundation of the game.

Immediately after the tires bumped the potholes, one of the teenagers would roll a hubcap past the driver's-side door in the same direction the car was going. The driver would see what he believed to be his hubcap rolling out in front of his car. Before he could think too much or get a good look at the hubcap, a different teenager would pick up the rolling hubcap and start running down the street with it.

Hubcap certainly did not always work, but when it did, it was worth the wait. It was perfect, because not only were male drivers of all ages the ones most likely to speed, but they were also the ones most susceptible to taking the bait. Once the driver was hooked, the entire neighborhood would enjoy the show. The kid running with the hubcap would cut across the snow-covered lawns and backyards of our unfenced neighborhood, careful to stay within sight of the driver.

The chase would involve other children of all ages pelting the passing car with piles of pre-made snowballs as the enraged driver, in his car with all four hubcaps, went sliding around the ice-covered streets. They were chasing a hubcap that wasn't even theirs and they were speeders, so in our minds they deserved everything they got. It was just our quaint little piece of Americana. I'm pretty sure Norman Rockwell had sketches of such scenes, but they're not among his most popular works.

Most often the drivers would eventually give up and drive away wondering what level of Dante's Hell they had driven into, but occasionally one would actually get out of his car to see which hub-cap was missing. Some drivers would remain angry as they walked around their entire vehicle and realized they were in possession of all four hubcaps. If we were lucky, they might yell at us kids that they had better things to do than play our silly games. Others would just blame themselves for being so foolish. They would jump back into their cars, not wanting to face the fact that they had been played.

However, the good ones smiled or chuckled as they got back into their cars and drove away shaking their heads, laughing at what had just happened. It was these rare drivers who really made me think about the different types of people in the world. The angry drivers seemed to be the *blame-others* type of people. The annoyed drivers seemed to be the *blame-yourself* kind of individuals. It was the third group, the *blame-nobody* folks, who seemed to embrace the "well, that's what you get" type of mentality; they seemed to be free to enjoy the entire experience.

The funny thing was, those drivers we had sucked into the game of Hubcap always seemed to drive more slowly through the neigh-borhood in the weeks and months that followed. It might have been out of fear, but it also might have been out of amusement. As a kid, I always felt like they were now part of the club. It seemed like they slowed down because we had all shared something together. I'm pretty sure some of them would smirk at us kids as they remem-bered their hubcap experience. Whether it's true or not, who knows, but I'm not sure it really matters.

Eventually, we ran out of new speeders to try to seduce into our game of Hubcap. The speeders who fell for it once certainly didn't fall for it twice. The speeders who saw through it from the get go continued to see through it each time we tried. Also, the speeders whose cars didn't have hubcaps were a problem. They must have found it odd that kids would run by them with a hubcap in their hands each time they came to our stop sign, but you can't blame us for trying.

Our once-useful hubcap, which rested in a place of prominence next to the O'Connell's milk box, eventually ended up rusting in the nearby window well. Experience proved that snowballs and water balloons seemed to have the opposite effect of making speeding drivers only go faster. Like much of life, the solution to the speeding drivers was there all along. We just needed to notice it.

As is the case in most parts of the world, the neighborhood congress of moms had a finely tuned awareness of "that's what you get." After watching the insanity of Uncle Jimmy and the game of Hubcap for a few months, they suggested their own solution. From lives of experience and a profound understanding of the human species, the moms added one word to the neighborhood constitution. It fixed the problem with speeding cars quickly and completely, without violence of any kind.

Of the innumerable amendments in the neighborhood's ever-changing constitution, one read, "All street hockey nets will be removed from the street quickly and courteously for *all* oncoming automobiles." Street hockey was an everyday happening, so this was a very important amendment that could not be changed without serious consideration. The congress of moms made the most minor of changes by adding the word *neighborhood* before the word *automobiles*. Now it only applied to cars from our own neighborhood.

"If they're not from the neighborhood, make them wait a little bit, especially if they're speeding," Pinky's mom declared to us all.

When the older kids took their sweet time to move the nets out of the way, the drivers lost all of the benefit of cutting through our neighborhood. When this happened to the drivers on a regular basis, they soon found their shortcut to be of little value. And boy did it work. This simple amendment to the constitution completely fixed the problem. The shortcut quickly became a longcut for non-neigh- borhood vehicles. Soon, neighborhood cars were the only ones driv- ing down our street. It was not only better for the safety of the chil- dren, but our street hockey games were interrupted far less often. It just goes to show how delicate "that's what you get" can be. I'm pretty sure Gandhi would have been proud as well.

It's funny how complicated we can make things. It's so simple once you see a solution, but until you see it, you simply don't. All the drivers were still doing what they do, and we were doing what we do. It was just a matter of noticing "what you get" when we're all doing what we do. Best of all, I still got to see those three kinds of people as they waited for the street hockey nets to be moved. Some still blamed others. Some still blamed themselves. A rare few blamed no one. It's the blame-no-one people who have always re- mained the most impressive to me, no matter where I meet them.

The speeding drivers who got caught in Hubcap, my Uncle Jim- my, the great Kmart caper, fishing with Ben, and the Pinky Revolt were experiences of the law of *that's what you get*—actions and con- sequences, a.k.a. *cause and effect.* In the end, it's really not at all per- sonal. Consequences are just life telling you "that's what you get." Even when it seems personal, it's really just life.

Isn't That Great

After daydreaming in the bookstore about my "that's what you get" childhood, I hopped on my bike to glide further down the hill to my favorite coffee shop, Pannikin. It's in a great old building that was a train station back in the 1920s. Its high ceilings and low floors provide a spacious feeling one doesn't seem to get from our modern buildings. The owners had converted it into a café and painted it bright yellow, which does seem to make any building look happier.

I was a bit shot from the day's adventures and thought a cup of coffee was warranted. I have a working hypothesis that enlightenment is found about halfway through the day's second cup of coffee, so let's just say I was looking forward to it. I never really drank coffee until I was in my thirties, and it's one of the few real regrets I have in life. I love coffee, and it's not a fleeting kind of love—it's a commitment I'm willing to make for the long haul. It's one of the two things in life I've run into that work as advertised, every time.

It wasn't until I was thirty-three that I had a good taste of "the devil's cup," as it was first called when it arrived in Europe. I could never stomach the standard supermarket coffee in a can that's made from Robusto coffee beans. It always made my intestines cramp.

Then one day my friend Mark produced a cup made from fresh Arabica coffee beans. It changed my life. I don't mean it changed my life the way those people on the infomercials say, "The Thigh Master changed my life." I mean coffee set me free from the biological tyranny of my circadian rhythms, and for that I am eternally grateful.

Within a month of discovering good coffee, I could be found reading *The Joy of Coffee* and downloading articles from the Specialty Coffee Association of America. Within three months, I had purchased my own coffee bean roaster and had found a supplier of green coffee beans. I ordered every kind coffee in the world and home roasted each variety of bean. The cup it produced was then tasted and rated by both my friends and myself.

Along the way I tested every type of coffee-making machine and device on the market. People are all just doing what they do, but that doesn't mean it isn't exhausting or insane. Eventually, I concluded that Indonesian coffees worked best for me in both taste and the smooth, pleasant state of agitation they provide. I was relieved when the self-imposed Arabica Project came to an end, but probably not as relieved as the people who know me.

I'm quite clear that everyone, and I do mean everyone, has their own absolutely unique perception of each moment in this thing we refer to as living. Had I listened to others' perceptions of coffee, I would be hunting down the expensive Kona coffee or getting on waiting lists for Jamaican Blue Mountain (overrated, by the way). But since I knew that my perception of each bean would be unique, I felt inclined to experience them all. When someone asks me what my favorite kind of coffee is, I'm not guessing like most people. I can say with certitude that an Indonesian bean with an Italian roast, made with an Aeropress, produces my favorite cup of coffee.

With no one waiting in line at Pannikin, I was quickly served an almond croissant and a lava-hot cup of their signature coffee, Indo Noir. I found a seat up on the second-floor balcony that overlooked both the patio and the street below. It would be three minutes before I burned my tongue and five minutes before I could actually drink my coffee, so I just sat nibbling at my croissant and enjoying the sights.

An old acquaintance, Wayne, spotted me, and we gave each other our now-customary courteous raise of our chins. Wayne's friends were forever fascinated by how much he could complain, so they started calling him Whine. They did so with a jovial smile, out loud, directly to him with the erroneous expectation that it might quell some of his constant complaining. The beauty of Wayne was that he was completely unaffected. His nickname wasn't even a speed bump on his superhighway of complaint-based living.

I never took Wayne's way of being personally. That's probably why I always called him by his actual name. He was just "passing the jelly" like everyone else. I realized early on that Wayne had a small design oddity that made him the way he was. You know how your bathroom sink has a little slot near the top to keep it from over-flowing? Well, Wayne was born without one of those, so his stuff just flowed out all over everybody.

Wayne didn't have an actual job, as far as I could tell. He was either a trustafundian or received some type of government check every month. He was in his forties with graying hair and a perpetual tension in his brow that only added to his already angular face. It made him look like he was forever at a police station line-up trying to identify a guy who had mugged him in a dark alley. Being the whitest guy on the planet, Wayne was often inspired to refer to his unrelenting negativity as his way of "just keepin' it real." This did add a much-needed comic relief of which I'm sure he was completely unaware.

Wayne also had a disturbingly stiff gate when he walked. You know how some dancers can move so gracefully that it looks like they are floating across the floor? Right, well Wayne was the exact opposite of that. Imagine the Hunchback of Notre Dame without the hunch. Throw in a year's worth of some intense physical therapy for your humpless Quasimodo and that would be Wayne walking toward you.

He was not physically deformed. It was the tightness of the muscles in his hips that had completely immobilized his pelvis. Each step forward required him to rotate his entire body by pivoting on his opposite foot. The pivot allowed his other foot to move forward, but it made him appear as though he was walking on a lazy Susan when he approached. I always felt for Wayne a little bit, as any forward progress made by him took much more effort than for other people.

"Some yoga or just plain stretching might help your sore back," I once recommended.

"I can't do yoga or stretching. I'm too tight," was Wayne's insightful reply.

"Yeah, that's the point," I said, dropping the entire topic into a conversational abyss.

Wayne had the amazing talent of being able to find the cloud in every silver lining. If he wasn't complaining about his back, then it was the president. If it wasn't the president, from either party, then it was the leader of some other country. Then there was always the environment. If it wasn't the environment, it was how much the phone companies make per call on the three pay phones left in the United States.

I found his level of negativity quite impressive. This was partly due to the fact that he appeared to be blessed with an infinite number of complaints, but also because I was blessed to not run into him very often. Whenever we would cross paths, I'd just mix up some Instant Compassion and things would go swimmingly.

My self-created formula for Instant Compassion is just like those instant cake-in-a-box products that Betty Crocker and the gang have been putting on the store shelves since the 1950s, except that you don't need to add an egg to mine. It's pretty simple, but let me walk you through it.

In a big bowl of "we're all human," all you do is ask and answer (for yourself) three simple questions. In this case we'll use Wayne as our subject.

"Did Wayne have any control over the genes he inherited or his early childhood conditioning that laid the foundation for *how* he is?" I sincerely asked myself.

"No, Wayne did not have any control over those things," I answered.

"Does Wayne, or any of us for that matter, control the perceptions, thoughts, feelings, and emotions that rise up into consciousness?" I genuinely inquired.

"Not really. None of us do, if you think about it," I concluded.

"Which would be worse: having to listen to Wayne or having to *be* Wayne?" I contemplated.

"Being Wayne would be far worse than having to listen to him," I realized.

After all three simple questions are asked and answered, there is nothing left to do but stir gently and repeat if necessary (like shampooing). When done just right, you can feel the compassion rise up from deep inside you. Try it sometime for real, and you'll be very impressed. It's free for now, but once I copyright it, you'll have to send me a dollar every time you use it.

Wayne's abilities and feats of negativity on this day were no exception from my previous encounters. I quickly whipped up a batch of Instant Compassion and was delighted that it turned out so fluffy. It seemed to be working exceptionally well. However, some of that good feeling might have been from the perfect bite of croissant I had just taken. It was the middle part where you hit the sweet almond paste, so we'll never really know for sure.

Wayne continued chatting at me as I excused myself and pulled out one of those little green plastic one-handed flossing things from my wallet that obviously need to be given a name of some kind.

"Ever since I had a crown put in on my upper right molar," I interjected, "I have to carry these little flossing things in my wallet because there's one little spot where food gets caught. A piece of almond is jammed in there right now."

Wayne was inhaling, so I took the opportunity to continue.

"The dentist who did my crown quit after his work on me to become a full-time horse dentist. I should have asked for references. When most of them said, 'Naaaaaaay,' I would have known to go somewhere else."

"You know, those plastic flossers are murder on the environment," was Wayne's only reply.

I took the opportunity to blatantly steal George Carlin's material and explained to Wayne that, for all we know, the only reason we humans are here on the planet is because the earth wanted some plastic. When Wayne didn't even chuckle, the soufflé of compassion that fluffed up so nicely over the first few moments of our time together suddenly collapsed. I remixed two new batches, but they just wouldn't rise.

I decided I had reached a point where a radically new approach to our acquaintanceship needed to be established. If Wayne wasn't going to laugh at my bad jokes—or at least acknowledge them—then I no longer felt obligated to listen to his constant complaining. We didn't have a written contract or even a verbal one for that matter, but still, a deal is a deal.

Since we live in a cause-and-effect world, I was wondering if there was some little monkey wrench I could toss into the gears of Wayne's complaint factory that might cause them to jam. Yup, everybody is just doing what they do, but that doesn't mean you can't try to change things that no longer serve you.

Creating change in people, myself included, is like a fishing expedition. You can't control whether the fish will actually bite, so you just have to keep casting your line out there at different times, and with different baits, to see what works. It was time to see what Wayne might bite on. He was already *very* taken with himself, so the bait had to be something out of the ordinary that would catch his attention.

I took a sip of coffee and a bite of croissant to make sure I had enough caffeine and sugar for my brain to be in an optimal state of functioning. Wayne was onto the thrilling topic of gasoline prices, so I was free to be on autopilot for a while. I realized that agreeing with him only made him complain more, but disagreeing with him also made him complain more. Remaining neutral seemed to lead to more complaining as well. Wayne had become a great riddle, wrapped in a paradox, with a decorative bow of enigma securing the entire package. I was excited about resolving such an interesting dilemma.

Wayne was so well manured that even the slightest tidbit of negativity would instantly sprout into some new dissatisfaction. It struck me that the only viable alternative was to envelope and embrace each of his expostulations in its entirety. I needed to joyfully swallow each complaint whole so there was nothing left. The total complaint-stopping technique I employed was ultimately very simple, but let me forewarn you: with great power comes great responsibility. Don't pull this one out lightly.

Wayne began to complain about the shade of tan that the city had chosen for the new sea wall. It didn't match the sandstone cliffs as well as he would have liked.

"Isn't that great," I interjected with a beaming smile.

"Did you hear what I said?" he replied.

"Yes. Isn't that great," I pleasantly stated again.

Wayne's brain stalled for a second, but he was a pro. He had a pile of other topics he could complain about.

"Yeah, what a disappointment that new restaurant on D Street is."

"Isn't that great," I said smiling.

"What?"

"Isn't that great," I insisted.

"Isn't what great?" Wayne asked in frustration.

I rose from my chair and reached over the round café table and grabbed the outsides of Wayne's shoulders with both hands.

"You're alive man. You are aliiiiiive!" I maniacally screamed. "Isn't that great."

I'm not going to lie. Wayne was slightly shocked.

"What are you doing?" Wayne whispered as he noticed people staring at us.

"You're alive, Wayne. You are experiencing life. All these things you complain about mean you're out there experiencing life. Isn't that great? As they say, 'it's much better than the alternative.'"

"I guess," Wayne conceded.

And then, as I've learned happens when this masterful technique is employed, Wayne had nothing to say. "Isn't that great" stopped all his complaining dead in its tracks. It was the monkey wrench that turned Whine back into Wayne. It's not turning water into wine, but it's still a pretty good trick.

A few weeks later I ran into Wayne. One simple "isn't that great" instantly jammed his complaint gears. And he's been that way ever since, at least with me. These days I'll get the courteous head nod or the friendly wave, but Wayne knows that "isn't that great" is much more than he is capable of dealing with. When you want to complain about dandelions to someone who sees them as wildflowers, you might as well go somewhere else.

"Isn't that great" performs a minor miracle each time I use it. Yes, everybody is doing what they do, and doing the best they can while they do it, but that doesn't mean you need to be around them while they are doing it. Feel free to try this technique on the complainers in your life, but be careful. It can really clear your social calendar, depending on who your friends are.

Wayne was on the other side of the café talking at some guy who seemed genuinely interested in the vast pay-phone conspiracy going on all across America. I remained free to roam the planet at will. I wandered into the retail section at Pannikin to purchase a pound of whole bean Indo Noir for home use. I loved this part of the café because it was so eclectic. You want some antique bowling pins? They've got 'em. A pink flamingo for your lawn? This is the place. Is Buddha, the Virgin of Guadalupe, a Christian or Gnostic cross on your shopping list? They're in the back left corner. Need a stovetop espresso maker or a clock that looks like a real bullfrog? Carol at the counter has got that covered, too.

I was enjoying the perfect chemical balance that a cup of coffee and a croissant can induce when my friend Topper spotted me in line. I could never get a straight answer as to why people called him Topper, but the name seemed to fit. He was a Tasmanian devil on ecstasy, the excitement of a circus coming to a dying town, a man like any other—only more so.

Topper told me once that he never read children's books growing up. He and his mom read Greek mythology instead. He was also a literature major in college and still reread all the great works in his spare time. I surmised that's why in Topper's world everything was big, exciting, full of potential, and full of drama. All things considered, Topper's way was probably not a bad way to go.

He could quote the great works of Western civilization at will, which made conversations with him interesting. What made those same conversations odd was that he didn't just weave the quotes into his everyday conversation, they were often the only thing that made up his conversation. He never told you he was quoting someone, but he spoke in a way that made it clear he was repeating someone else's words. He'd walk you through much of the Western canon over the course of a lengthy chat. My love of quotes since I was a child made Topper one of my favorite people to talk to, but there was something odd about his way that I could never quite put my finger on.

When I spoke with Topper, I'd always try to recognize as many quotes as I could and give myself a point for each one I knew. My current record was twelve, which I'd set a while back at a New Year's Eve party. Topper never got bored with hearing himself talk, so it was a fun game for all involved, even though he didn't know he was playing. Plus, I had the added pleasure of trying to figure out what he was actually saying. The quotes were often vague references to the actualities of whatever topic we were discussing, so you were never really sure exactly what Topper meant. I felt like a tourist in a foreign land trying to decipher directions given by a local. Very stimulating stuff.

Topper was also an original thinker in his own right. For instance, he drifted off into his own little universe so often that he would tend to run out of gas in his car on a regular basis. Most people would figure out a way to remember to look at the gas gauge more often. Not Topper. He eventually solved the problem by having an extra gas tank installed in his SUV. He felt this would at least cut his problem in half, which it did. It's that kind of unorthodox thinking that I find truly inspiring.

"Ahoy, and other nautical expressions," was Topper's greeting, quoting the Dodo from *Alice in Wonderland*.

"Hey, Topper," I said, "How's your new restaurant on D Street going?"

"I've been working like a horse and eating like a hog and sleeping like a dead man," he said, "but happy is the man who can make a living by his hobby."

It appeared that Topper was working hard, but loved what he was doing. I knew the horse, hog, and dead man was from Rudyard Kipling. I couldn't place the second half, but I was already up to two points, which was a good start.

"How's the family?" I asked.

"Hell hath no fury like a woman scorned," Topper answered, raising his eyebrows and smiling. "And it's beginning to smell like the left wing of the day of judgment."

Topper and his wife Karen had been unhappily married for years and were in the process of getting a divorce. Like many divorces, it had apparently deteriorated into the ugliness that had been going on for quite a while. The three kids they co-created were the ones caught between these two so-called adults doing what they do. The Shakespeare quote was so common that I almost didn't take a point, but I couldn't get the second quote about judgment day, so three points was the new total.

"How are your kids?"

"Mother *is* the name for God in the lips and hearts of little children."

First, I had no idea where Topper's quote came from, but more important, I felt like he was kidding himself that losing the hearts of his kids to his wife wasn't killing him. Topper used to light up when quoting his kids. It sounded from our conversation like he might even being losing them in a court battle of some kind.

"What are you doing about it?" I asked.

"Shakespeare is the happy hunting ground of all minds that have lost their balance," Topper replied.

The quote was from James Joyce's *Ulysses*. I never would have known, but he'd used it last year at the New Year's Eve party. I'd liked it so much that I looked it up on New Year's Day, so I now had a total of four points. His solution to losing his kids was apparently to sit around and read Shakespeare. I was intrigued and saddened by Topper's resignation to the situation he was in. He was normally full of innovative options for himself, yet seemed at a loss when it came to his wife and kids.

To me this situation was no different than if his car had run out of gas. If I could help out I would, but it needed to be done just right—like all things, I suppose. Topper always seemed interesting and upbeat, but one only had to scratch the surface to uncover his very strong desire to be right. Like most people, he had his own perceptions of things, and he was sticking to them. He had been known to browbeat others into intellectual submission, but he tended to do so with a smile. I found him interesting enough to put up with a fair bit of it, especially when he could shift my point of view on a topic I was pretty firm on.

This is why I loved being at Pannikin. You could go from one extreme to the other when dealing with the people here. Wayne had his complaint gears buzzing at full speed, and I had tossed a monkey wrench into them for my sake. Topper, on the other hand, had a monkey wrench stuck in his gears that I wanted to help him get out, for his good and the good of his family. Plus, if he was already pulling quotes from James Joyce, then the odds of me getting many more points weren't very good. He would soon be diving into books that weren't even available in *CliffsNotes*.

"Yeah, I hear you, Topper," I began. "I think it was Sigmund Freud who said, 'Perhaps the best thing that can happen to children is to have their parents hate each other. It's the relationship they'll be emulating for the rest of their lives, so it's wonderful to have that as a foundation.'"

"Freud didn't say that," Topper corrected.

"Oh, I guess you're right. It would be absurd to think that, wouldn't it?" I replied.

Topper got to be right, and with the leverage of his kids, I got to wiggle loose the monkey wrench a bit.

"We'll just keep using our attorneys until things work themselves out," Topper added. "What else can you do?"

He wasn't speaking in quotes. His tone had shifted. I was actually having a conversation with Topper, which I must admit, seemed strange.

"Yep," I mused, "I think it was Einstein who said, 'Doing the same thing over and over again and expecting a different result is a sign of genius."

"He said that was a sign of insanity, not genius," Topper corrected.

He was onto my game, but he just couldn't help himself.

"You're right, aren't you, it was insanity he was talking about, wasn't it?"

"But it's hard. Whenever I get the chance, I just want to get back at her for all the trouble she's caused me."

"I totally get that. I think that's probably why Jesus said, 'Revenge is a dish best served cold'" (I knew Topper went to church on occasion).

"Jesus didn't say that," he chuckled.

"You're right, I probably mixed him up with someone else."

Under the right circumstances you can get a lot of leverage with Jesus. The monkey wrench was almost out.

"It's hard, though," Topper confided. "I'm at a point where I just hate Karen."

"Wasn't it your buddy, Oscar Wilde, who said, 'Hatred is the anger of the truly empowered'?"

"It's 'Hatred is the anger of the impotent,'" Topper offered.

He just couldn't help correcting me even though he was arguing against his own position. People are fascinating.

"Well, then maybe there's some type of 'divorce Viagra' that would help you and Karen come together in ways you haven't tried yet," I said.

"All right, all right." Topper said with a slight smile of appreciation. "I get it. I need to figure out a way for Karen and me to start speaking again."

"Get what? I was just sharing some of my favorite quotes."

"Well, thanks anyway," Topper mumbled.

The monkey wrench was out, at least temporarily.

"The wind sits in the shoulder of my sail," Topper added.

With clasped hand on brim of cap, he bowed his head, as any good Shakespearian would. Topper then turned with an appreciative wave of his hand and headed into the café. As he walked away, I was just thankful he wasn't wearing a leotard. His last quote meant he was back into his regular literary way of being and that I had earned one more point to bring my game total to five. Five was a pretty respectable showing.

I've learned to never underestimate a person's desire to be right. With certain types, letting them be right is the only way you can ever help them. I figured I had the right to be wrong, and Topper had the right to be right; I mean, what could be wrong with that, right? The best part, and the fun part, is if you can actually help someone while your two mutual insanities collide.

I have to admit, it felt pretty good to get Topper to at least step back and reassess what he was doing, since what he was doing didn't seem to be working too well. Plus, I've always agreed with Oscar Wilde's "Hatred is the anger of the impotent." Topper just needed to see that he wasn't stuck in neutral.

Funny thing about words—they're often an impotent tool when it comes to shifting someone's behavior. When used rationally, words can play like white noise in the background of our ongoing lives. When used judgmentally, words become the enemy to be defended against. That's why, when trying to effect change in others, I'll often use words in a way that's absurd.

In life, absurdity is a powerful tool. It grabs the human psyche in a way like nothing else, and when done well, reflects back on an absurdity you are trying to point out. When done poorly, people may be confused but are generally unharmed and no worse off than before. As far as approaches to change go, it's a pretty good one.

"Reality" is a word that is only properly spelled with quotation marks on each end, since most of *what is* is wrapped in a big story of our own perceptions. Those perceptions can change if you are willing to cast out enough lines, with enough different baits. I guess the fun part is in never knowing which bait will do the trick.

The Po Perspective

With the day's second cup of coffee in my body and a pound of whole bean Indo Noir in my hand, I walked out of Pannikin with noticeably more pep in my step than when I had entered. I arrived at my bike and perused the community bulletin board with flyers for yoga instructors, personal trainers, various religious instruction, schools of all kinds, surfing lessons, meditation groups, and much more. As I pedaled away I realized that most lives consist of a strange mixture of teachers and teachings whose influence is often recognized only in hindsight. I thought back and contemplated the notion that had it not been for a couple of Shaolin monks living in China and a millionaire bootlegger from West Egg, New York, my perspective on life and living could be drastically different.

I met the monks one night when I was seven years old. It was one of those rare moments where the doorway to a new way of being opens up for you—and best of all, you know it. The TV show was *Kung Fu*, and the voice coming from the television seized my attention.

"It is said a Shaolin priest can walk through walls. Looked for, he cannot be seen. Listened for, he cannot be heard. Touched, he cannot be felt."

Sign me up! I thought to myself. Shave my head and brand my little forearms with dragon logos. For my entire seven years on this planet, this is what I'd been looking for.

I wasn't a comic book kind of kid. That superhero stuff never did much for me, but these Shaolin monks really turned my crank. They were real people with real skills. Watching the old blind master fend off multiple attackers with only a wooden staff was riveting. How could I not want to be a guy who would always do his best to live in peace, but who could also open a can of whup-ass on anyone when he needed to? Right away I knew being an ass-kicking sage was the way to go.

My favorite scenes were always the flashbacks of young Caine receiving esoteric lessons on the multiple meanings of life. The mesmerizing elder monks, Master Kan and the blind Master Po, demonstrated their power through a centered and wisdom-filled perspective on living. I'd never seen anything like it.

I can still remember sitting on the scratchy green couch in my living room, eating brownie batter with a wooden spoon and watching *Kung Fu*. The combination of sickly sweet brownie batter and the deep esoteric teachings of a Buddhist master is a very powerful combination that is not soon forgotten. The sugar rush to my brain permanently seared the following exchange into my prefrontal cortex:

Master Po: "Do you hear the grasshopper at your feet?"
Young Caine: "Old man, how is it that you hear these things?"
Master Po: "Young man, how is it that you do not?"

Oh man, if there was a Shaolin temple in my town, I would have hopped on my bike and signed up for their Sunday School, catechism, or whatever classes they had for kids. On my own, I wasn't even wise enough to realize that, once again, I was going to feel horrible after eating sixteen ounces of raw brownie batter. Deep down I knew that I needed some serious Shaolin teaching to have any chance at all in this life.

I did ask around, and there were no Shaolin temples to be found in my town or the next town over. I was out of luck when it came to being trained by a master, and despite my many requests, my mom would not let me get my head shaved.

However, like any other seven year old, I was free to pretend I was Master Po. Pretending you are an old, blind, Chinese monk with a shaved head did make for some transcendent times. First, my frog-catching skills down at the swamp improved immensely when I was Master Po. Second, punishments from my parents involving silence or restriction became rather enjoyable when I remembered the secret of being Master Po. Overall, I found life as Master Po very appealing.

When in Po mode I would see someone come into my room, but being blind, I would be impressed that my Shaolin skills had allowed me to detect their presence. I was thrilled again that I could miraculously identify who it was. I would turn to them and say their name in a way that indicated they should be surprised by my feat of sibling identification.

"What?" was the usual response from my underimpressed relatives.

When I became Master Po, my parents would be referred to as Mother and Father instead of Mom and Dad. This was done out of respect for my elders. It was also done in such a pleasant and soft tone that my parents didn't seem to mind that I was blind, bald, and Chinese.

I didn't permanently become Master Po, but for a day or two after seeing an episode of *Kung Fu*, my family was in for a heavy dose.

It was amazing how peaceful I felt simply by pretending to be so wise. I had real compassion for all of those around me. My deeply grounded pretend wisdom allowed me to see that others just didn't understand the way of the world.

As a true Shaolin wannabe, when someone asked me a question, there was no straightforward answer. An answer was given only after a long pause and with a hint of Chinese sage accent.

"How did you do that?" a sibling might ask.

"As the tiger hunts and the crane flies," I would reply after a long silence.

"Why are you doing that?" adults would inquire.

"Does the rain need a reason to fall?" I would ask in return, which confused them enough that there was a good chance they would just walk away.

People, especially in my part of the world, tended to ask themselves, "What would Jesus do?" A rare few might ask, "What would Buddha do?" I even know a few folks in Austin, Texas, who ask, "What would Willie Nelson do?" At age seven, I tended to ask myself, "What would Master Po do?"

This went on for years. The most confusing part for my parents, siblings, and friends was that I never told anyone when I was being Master Po. If other kids were pretending to be Spider-Man or Superman they would tell you that's who they were or at least they'd have a cape tied around their neck as a clue. However, it was clear to me that Master Po would never tell you he was Master Po. He would just *be* Master Po.

"Why were you and Ben playing with matches in the woods this afternoon?" my father asked me one day (for very good reason).

I tilted my head and inhaled thoughtfully through my nostrils.

"Why not?" I replied in a slowed-pace and sagely tone.

Let's just say my reply was unappreciated, but I found the paradox of punishments handed down to Ben and me to be very intriguing. I got grounded for two weeks. My fellow pyromaniac Ben gave no such reply to his mom, yet he received the punishment that a sage would have handed down. Ben's mom made him build and tend a fire in the middle of their gravel driveway, every day, until he was so sick of fires that he begged to be released from the unbearable sentence. My desire to flirt with the flame smoldered within for years to come. Ben's was extinguished by his own hand.

Being Master Po affected me in many enjoyable ways, but I did notice that it sometimes seemed to have the opposite effect on those around me. Funny how imagining yourself to be an old Chinese guy changes the way you interact with people. Others often left me alone when I was Master Po. This was a wonderful benefit when living in a large family, but I was looking for a little more out of life than to just be left alone. This is where the other strange bedfellow in the creation of my beingness came into play.

His name was Jay Gatsby. Yes, that would be The Great Gatsby, from F. Scott Fitzgerald's book by the same name. I wish I could say that I was a child prodigy at age seven and was reading all the great works of Western literature, but that would be a big, fat lie, and I'm trying to avoid doing that. It's really because the movie *The Great Gatsby* was made in Newport, Rhode Island, when I was about seven years old. My mother was hired to be one of the extras in the movie, and it was very exciting for everyone in the neighborhood. She had her long hair cut short to look like a 1920s flapper, and she got to wear funny hats and dresses from the time period. It was memorable for the entire family because she had to leave the house at 4 a.m. for a few weeks, so we all had to make our own breakfast.

About a year after my mother was done hanging out with Robert Redford, the entire family went to the movie theatre to search for Mom in the giant party scenes. As a seven year old, I was very unclear about which 1920s flapper was my mother. Twice in what seemed like a twelve-hour movie, my entire family simultaneously pointed at a distant shot of a crowded party playing on the screen.

"That's Mom, did you see her?" they would all declare, but I couldn't tell one flapper from the next.

Apparently, the movie was such a success that they made a book out of it. We naturally purchased a copy of *The Great Gatsby* when it came out. We left it on the coffee table in the family room. This was just in case absolutely everyone who entered the house wanted to know that my mother was in a Hollywood movie. Perhaps it was my guilt over not spotting my mother on a crowded movie screen in less than one second that made me pick up the book so often.

I'll be honest, to a seven year old the book was even less appealing than the movie. It had no pictures and had very small print. For my mother's sake, I gave it a real effort. I muscled through the first six lines of the book on numerous occasions:

> In my younger and more vulnerable years my father gave me some advice that I've been turning over in my mind ever since.
>
> "Whenever you feel like criticizing anyone," he told me, "just remember that all the people in this world haven't had the advantages that you've had."

Most often, I read these first six lines of *The Great Gatsby* out loud. For some reason, hearing the words seemed to help me get the gist of what Fitzgerald was saying. I was pretty sure it meant that I shouldn't be mean to other people because they might have had a hard life.

I'll admit that from line seven onward, I found Fitzgerald a bit wordy. Each time I would read those first six lines with great optimism, but then at line seven the temperature gauge in my brain would hit the red zone. At line eight, the radiator would blow. At line nine, the entire engine would seize. Line ten was just a tempting mirage on a long-deserted highway that, in my heart of hearts, I knew I would never really reach.

I was about to give up on the rest of the text, but realized I might as well try and read the last page as well. I was pretty sure if you read the very beginning and the very end of a book, that was pretty close to having read the whole thing. I fanned through the entire text to make sure there weren't any pictures I had missed and arrived at the last page.

Phewww, I thought as I tried to understand what the heck this writer was talking about. Oddly, only reading the first six lines of the book hadn't allowed me to understand the last page. In desperation, I jumped to the very last line of the book. I found it quite interesting. It was a nice little sentence about a boat and the current that I read aloud a few times. I liked boats. I liked water. It was interesting.

Over the next few days I grew genuinely curious about what the last line of my mother's movie meant. Then one day I walked to school early and went directly to the library. Mrs. McGowen, the school librarian, was sitting at her desk when I arrived. She was a middle-aged woman with her hair pulled tight into a big bun on the back of her head. She also had those perfect librarian glasses that hung around her neck, always ready to be called into action.

Like most librarians I've met along the way, she was helpful with an urgency that made you feel important. I'm convinced that librarians might be the best self-esteem tonic there is. If you are ever feeling down, just go ask a librarian some random question like what the GNP of Albania is and watch them spring into action. Helping you answer your question becomes their personal mission. It's so much more inspiring than a Google search.

I stood next to Mrs. McGowen and placed my opened copy of *The Great Gatsby* on her desk. I pointed to the last line of the book.

"What does this mean?" I asked.

I had no idea that there have been untold lectures given and papers written about this one line. I think Mrs. McGowen did know this because there was a long and respectful pause before she answered. I stood silent until she took my hand and read the last line out loud, so I could hear it read properly.

"And so we beat on, boats against the current, borne ceaselessly into the past."

I'd never seen someone read words in this way unless they were reading the Bible. There was a reverence as she spoke them like she was being transported somewhere. She had completely changed from her normal way of being, just like I did when I was Master Po.

"It means we can't escape our past. No matter how hard we try, we carry our past with us into our future," she said calmly.

Mrs. McGowen then sat silently. Her eyes glazed over. I could tell she was being swept away in a flood of important memories from her life. It was like she wasn't there anymore, which was strange for this woman who was always there for everybody. That last line of *The Great Gatsby* had a major effect on her, but I couldn't quite tell if it was good or bad. I waited as she drifted back into the present.

"If you like famous quotes," Mrs. McGowen said, "we have books full of them over in the reference section. And the town library has an even better collection."

She walked me over and pointed out the books that she explained were just like dictionaries except that they were for quotes. If you had a word and you wanted a quote, all you had to do was look it up in one of these secret books. I was blown away and immediately saw how I could use these books as a major tactical advantage within my family. Everybody in my family except my brother was bigger than I was. Everybody except my brother had more years of school than I did. However, I could use the well-spoken words of others in the slaying of my siblings and in my own defense against my parents.

I had a rough idea of what Mrs. McGowen meant about the Gatsby quote, but my understanding wasn't solid. As a seven year old, I was very curious about not being able to escape under the weight of my long and colored past. It haunted me (but only in the Halloween kind of way, not the adult kind).

I often read the last line of my mother's movie out loud as I sat on our green scratchy couch and thought of how it had affected Mrs. McGowen. One day as I watched *Kung Fu*, Caine had a flashback to the blind Master Po.

Young Caine: Is it good to seek the past, Master Po? Does it not rob the present?

Master Po: If a man dwells on the past, then he robs the present.

But if a man ignores the past, he may rob the future.

The seeds of our destiny are nurtured by the roots of our past.

Master Po's words made clear for me the last line of *The Great Gatsby*. I understood how roots and seeds of the past are part of what grows into the future. I'd been planting sunflower seeds for years and watched them grow to ten feet tall.

Master Po, F. Scott Fitzgerald, and I were one. As far as I could tell, I now had a small but valuable clue about the esoteric nature of the world. I was very excited about it. Of course, my new understanding would soon be tested in the treacherous arena of life, specifically at the family dinner table.

Dinner at my home was a very predictable affair. Every week-night at 5:15 my dad pulled into the driveway from work, and every night at 5:30 we would eat dinner. Being Irish, my Mom thought a potato was a spice, so every night on my dinner plate would be a baked potato. The potato was accompanied by vegetables from a can and some kind of cooked but unseasoned meat. We would then say grace in unison, our voices as bland as the food we were about to consume.

"Dear Lord, thank you for the bounty we are about to receive. Amen."

The eating would commence once we had all been given ample time to apply the food "first aid" of salt and margarine in large doses to whatever was on our plate. Then the well-intended interrogation would begin.

"What did you learn at school today?" my father would alternately ask each of his five children.

If you didn't have an answer, you had to go look up a word in the dictionary and tell everyone what it meant. Most nights I had plenty of time to prepare an answer. My sisters and brother were seated closer to my dad, so they were usually quizzed before I was. They would spout off some random fact they had been taught that day, while I had time to cull the deep recesses of the day's learning and pick a plum.

Once again, my father's powers of perception were more powerful than I had suspected. He sensed the shift in my core understanding of the human experience that had taken place since the last time we had eaten baked potatoes together. On this night, I was the first child he turned to in search of an all-important new factoid. I couldn't think of anything to say, and I didn't feel like looking up a word in the dictionary, so I blurted out the words I had read out loud at least fifty times over the last month.

"We're all boats against the current, ceaselessly borne into the past,"

The response to my words was overwhelming. People turned and looked at me in a way I'd never really experienced. They were wide-eyed. They were shocked. Most important, they were silent.

The spouting of my stolen words had caused a response of awe and admiration from everyone at the dinner table. In a family of seven, you had to find your niche, and mine was apparently going to have to be that of a plagiarist. However, seconds later my oldest sister turned state's evidence against me. She was in Mr. Pelequin's advanced freshman English class and had just completed a book report on our family's favorite novel.

"That's from the end of *The Great Gatsby*," she announced to the entire table.

"Yes, we know, but it's still wonderful," my mom said.

"He doesn't even know what it means," my sister announced.

"I do, too, know what it means," I insisted.

My sister wasn't buying it. She had a firm motto when it came to her siblings: don't trust, and always verify.

"Really, then tell everybody what it means," she jeered.

My moment of glory was crashing and burning with each passing second. I had no idea what to say. A vision of Mrs. McGowen flashed inside my head, but I couldn't grasp her words. All I could see was her sitting silently at her desk thinking about the past. I panicked through another split second of blankness. Then an image of Master Po arose in my mind and I became a bald, blind, Chinese man as I had done so many times before. A blank, wide-eyed stare met my sister.

"It means the seeds of our past grow into our future," I said, in the slowed and compassionate cadence of a sage.

It wasn't exactly what Master Po had said, but it was close enough. Everyone at the table was in shock, again. I was more stunned than anyone, but hid it behind my sagely demeanor. It was like I'd won at the impossible carnival game where one in a thousand people will actually toss a softball into a doctored milk jug. You know it happens; you just never expect it to be you.

The immense power of words was demonstrated for me, by me, with a lot of help from Master Po and F. Scott Fitzgerald. And it had occurred at one of the most important fulcrums of power for a seven year old—the family dinner table. Thus, a lover of words was born.

The family dinner table was a pretty easy system to exploit at first. Within each family there are phrases that are repeated ad nauseam. I would notice these and go look up quotes for their key words. If I needed help, I would just ask a librarian. They would lend me their expertise with great enthusiasm. I'm pretty sure they found my desire to look up random quotes both inspiring and odd. The quotes most often involved history, work, knowledge, or learning, so no school psychologists were called in to assess my psyche.

"He who hesitates is lost," my dad would spout.

"Fools rush in where angels fear to tread," I offered only once and caused a panicked silence at the table.

"The early bird gets the worm," my mom would remind us.

"But the early worm gets eaten," I'd add to the delight of all.

"Neither borrower or lender be," was a family favorite.

"For loan oft lose both itself and friend," I'd throw in as real crowd pleaser (this still works as an adult, by the way).

"This above all: to thine own self be true," was my mom's all-time favorite quotation. It was usually offered when it came to making a difficult life decision. I later found out that her quote was not only from the same author, and the same book, but from the same paragraph as my dad's line about borrowers and lenders.

"But one must first 'know thyself,'" was my insightful reply.

Mrs. McGowen saved me a great deal of research by giving me the *know thyself* reply right off the top of her head. She didn't even have to look it up. She told me it was carved into some Greek temple at the "belly button" of the world, but I thought it was good anyway.

Along the way, I discovered that Einstein quotes are highly effective. Any sentence that starts with the words "Einstein said" is pretty intimidating to the average person. Most people aren't willing to argue with the smartest guy in the world. President Kennedy was pretty good too. To Irish Catholics he ranked just above the Pope in importance, so he was a good bet. Mark Twain and Will Rogers were also favorites because they were G-rated, but made fun of a lot of things.

The wise words of others were also useful when trying to talk my way out of delicate situations. I had two options when I thought I might need a good quote in the future. I would either go to school early or ride my bike after school to the town library. Since parents in my neighborhood assumed their kids were okay unless they heard otherwise, it was pretty easy to sneak off to the library whenever I wanted.

One day at school Hanky Carlson smeared a piece of watermelon into the back of my neck and I got a note sent home from my teacher. I allegedly retaliated by smashing a piece of watermelon onto the top of his head. Despite Hanky's inability to produce any corroborating witnesses, I was found guilty on all charges.

"Two wrongs don't make a right," Mr. O'Donnell spoke as he wrote out a note to my father.

I'd heard my father say those same words many times. I knew he wasn't going to be happy about a note from my teacher, but I didn't have time to go to the library and find an appropriate quote to use in my own defense. The best and only quote resource we had at home was a copy of *Strong's Bible Concordance*, which was basically a giant index of the Bible. My Great Aunt Mary had given it to us two years earlier as a Christmas gift, and it had sat entirely unused on our basement bookshelf ever since.

"Two wrongs don't make a right," my father said after reading my teacher's note.

"But it says in the Bible, 'Vengeance *is* mine; I will repay, saith the Lord.'"

Quoting God was a pretty bold move in my house, even bolder than quoting Einstein. My father's teeth clenched. He audibly exhaled out his nose in frustration. He stared at me for one, two, then five seconds. My words stunned him enough that he completely forgot about punishing me.

"Don't do it again," he said. His eyes were wide, and he had a heavy dose of frustration in his voice. We both knew that the God quote had thrown him off. Though intense, I thought it was great. It meant he probably wouldn't want to bring up anything associated with this incident ever again.

Over time, I became more than a little quote obsessed. I realized you could find a quote for any side of an argument you want to make. I was fascinated by the pursuit of the many varied perspectives on just about any issue I could think of. There was the profound angle, the funny angle, the angry angle, the sad angle, and just about any other angle you wanted. Quotes really made you think about things, even if it was just a little bit.

Every time I went to the library, I would grab the big quote books and read through them. When I was young, I'd skip most of the long quotes. I'd read the one or two liners. If they were really good, I'd write them down in my Dr. Seuss Notebook, Quotebook, Look-What-I-Wrote Book. If it seemed like something Master Po would say, then I would often write it down even if I didn't understand it. Then at night, between throwing balls of rolled up socks at my snoring brother, I would read my favorite quotes.

I kept my quote-filled notebooks under my mattress for easy access. I know most young boys would use this prime, under-the-mattress hiding spot for the dirty magazine they had pulled out of the neighbor's trashcan, but frankly, I was above such things. That, and the fact that my friend Chris's dad practically left his *Playboy* magazines lying around for us to look at whenever we wanted.

Chris's dad never came out and actually gave us permission to look at his Playboys. We had more of an unspoken agreement about the whole affair. He just casually left them in his home office where anyone could happen upon them. We happened upon them in the locked third filing cabinet from the left, second drawer down, in the very back. He also left the key practically in plain sight, by putting it in a white ceramic mug on the very top of his bookshelf. It was effortlessly obtained by moving the chair in his office up against the wall and standing on its arms.

I'll admit that the signs granting us permission were subtle. Chris and I held a closed-door meeting and assessed the situation. By unanimous vote we decided that it was okay with his dad if we looked at his Playboys whenever we wanted. However, we were raised to be respectful, so we never did it when his parents were home. We also understood that it was just common courtesy to always put them back *exactly* as we had found them.

The compilations of quotes kept under my mattress benefited more than just my family members. Teachers seemed to enjoy a well-turned phrase even more than blood relatives. Friends my age didn't seem to appreciate quotes at all, so I tended to spare them my witticisms.

My elementary school principal, Mr. Kruskowskus, seemed especially appreciative of my tendency to spout quotes. "Mr. K.," as we called him, was a stout man with an optimistic bounce in his step as he moved through the halls of Newman Elementary School. His sincerity was clear to all he encountered. He knew the name of every child in his school. It was this simple sign of caring that made him approachable to kids of all ages, shapes, and sizes.

Mr. K. was at the top of the educational food chain, so he could pretty much do whatever he wanted. He regularly wandered into the various classrooms during the week to interact with the kids. His main method of engaging us was to give a brief and often completely random lesson. It's thanks to a presentation he gave my sixth grade class that I never confuse the words "principle" and "principal." He explained to us all that the principal of the school was always your "pal." In his case it was actually true, which might be why I remember it.

One day Mr. K. turned up in my-sixth grade class to be the host for the yearly spelling bee. I considered myself a very good student, but I was aware that spelling was the weakest of all my subjects. The going was rough. In the third round I misspelled some commonly used word like "callipygian," and I was out of the competition. I took it pretty gracefully, but I thought I might redeem myself by quoting Mark Twain.

"I don't give a damn for a man who can only spell a word one way," I told Mr. K. and the entire class.

"You've just been awarded sweeping duty," Mr. K. said matter-of-factly, despite a slight smirk on his face.

This meant a sentence of hard labor for my impolite transgression. I would be forced to sweep the asphalt parking lots, pathways, and play areas with a broom for an entire recess period. It could have been worse, so I kept my mouth shut for the rest of the spelling bee.

Mr. K. understood that manual labor was a supremely effective way of disciplining students. It wasn't personal for Mr. K. He wouldn't hold it against me in the future. It was just another lesson in "that's what you get," another brilliantly designed demonstration of cause and effect.

There was no talking allowed during sweeping duty. My fellow elementary school convicts and I had but one thing to do: bear in mind our transgressions and the consequences that had followed them. By the way, Mr. K. also had the cleanest schoolyard in the entire state at no additional cost to the taxpayers.

Kids all around us were having fun as we went about our penance. I could have been out there enjoying a variety of games that tended to share the common benefit of completely exhausting their participants in a very short period of time. We would then be capable of sitting still in class and actually learning something.

While my transgression with Mr. K. seemed clear to everyone in class, it remained slightly unclear to me. I had dropped many quotes on him and other teachers in the past, and I had always escaped unscathed. Even when the quotes were a bit risqué, I'd always avoided punishment.

In one instance, I had neglected to do my officially assigned homework because I was doing extracurricular studies in chemistry and physics. I had spent the entire previous afternoon successfully designing, building, and testing a tennis-ball cannon with my friends. We produced a workable prototype using only duct tape, a tennis ball can with a hole in it, and some rubbing alcohol. We were learning a great deal until Mrs. Harrison saw a flaming tennis ball land on her lawn and confiscated our fuel supply.

"Mark Twain said, 'I have never let my schooling interfere with my education.'" I said in my own defense; no punishment followed.

I also neglected to write a year-end paper on what I would be doing over the summer. My reasoning at the time was that I couldn't see into the future, so why bother? Duh. Instead of doing the assignment, I went to Mrs. McGowen and together we found the perfect quote.

"Einstein said, 'I never think of the future—it comes soon enough,'" I told Miss Reeves, and she was so impressed that she let me write the paper over the weekend with no punishment at all.

I'd even escaped severe punishment when my "greatest fifth grade science fair entry ever to be created by an elementary school student, anywhere in the history of the entire world" failed so miserably that I left it at home. I was basically attempting to build an IBM mainframe computer with four D batteries, some telephone wire, and a really neat box my work boots came in. Needless to say, it didn't go quite as planned.

When I had nothing to show on science fair day, I purposely walked to school twenty minutes early to go look up quotes on failure at the library. Miss Reeves naturally asked me where my entry was when there was a big blank space on the table that had my name on it.

"W.C. Fields, said, 'If at first you don't succeed, try, try, and try again. Then give up. There's no use being a damned fool about it,'" was my cheerful reply.

Miss Reeves was kind enough to give me an "N" for "not satis-factory" on the project, the lowest possible grade, but there was no sweeping duty.

I couldn't figure out why my current quotation to Mr. K. had led me to be sweeping the pavement. Then I realized that the times I did not get punished, I had always used the name of a famous person and *then* said the quote attributed to them. This time I had said the quote with no reference attached. I knew I wasn't being punished for plagiarism, so what else could it be?

I swept a while longer until I realized that referencing a well-known person actually changed the adult's perspective on what was being said. It changed my words from those of a wise-ass kid mouth-ing off to the words of wisdom from a source that warranted their respect, consideration, or at least amusement. How they experienced the exact same words depended entirely on who they thought was saying them. Without my noting the source, Mr. K. experienced me as a smart-aleck who needed to sweep some pavement.

I continued sweeping and dropped into Po mode. I watched with great interest as the grains of sand and dirt tumbled over each other. Each push of the broom was its own little event in time. What I was doing could be viewed as manual labor or as a spiritual exercise. It didn't matter one whit to the sand or the broom which way I chose.

My mind drifted, and I recalled the sand funnel at the Boston Museum of Science and the tumbling cause-and-effect world we live in. In the short view, I realized that had I not said my Mark Twain quote to Mr. K., I wouldn't be sweeping at all. In the long view, had I not turned on *Kung Fu* five years ago and my mother not been the starring extra in *The Great Gatsby*, I probably wouldn't be sweeping the pavement due to my love of quotes. But, it was only because of my love for Master Po that I was able to experience sweeping duty differently from how most others experienced it.

I was then struck by the obvious: being Master Po was really just a change in perspective, and the reason I liked quotes so much is that they show some of the different perspectives that the same exact situation can be viewed from. My love of quotes was found in the joy that came from the shift in perspective so often provided by a well-placed string of words. Someone, potentially anyone, could change their perspective on a situation if the right words were applied at the right time.

A blister began to rise up on the second knuckle of my index finger. I paused to look at it and thought about the fact that I could be playing with my friends right now had I been able to spell. I wouldn't be growing blisters and contemplating the great mystery of life.

Now there's an odd word, *mystery*, I thought. Why wouldn't they just spell it *mistery* or *mistory*, like it was a missed story. Or why not spell it *mystory*? Oh, that's funny. Maybe life is a big mystery because most of it is just my story.

My short life had already been full of stories. It was an adventure, a comedy, a tragedy, a rollercoaster ride, a battle, a prison sentence, a celebration, a mission, a spiritual journey. In later years I could see that life, for all of us, was at times an opera, a country western song (same as an opera, only shorter), a terminal sexually transmitted disease, an epic romantic journey, a hero's quest. But it's all still "my story."

I looked down again as I swept and wondered what "my story" really was. Maybe I was a simple grain of sand caught in the unending chain of cause and effect; or maybe I was a miraculously unique experiencing of life that would never again be repeated throughout all time. Then I realized that on the good days, I'm both at the same time. Of course, that's just my story, but I'm sticking to it.

Shady Grady

What a day it had been. Everybody was out there just doing what they do, which for most people isn't much to get excited about, yet I can't help but be immensely intrigued by the entire process.

My time at the coffee shop had gotten me cranked up and tanked up for the long uphill pedal home. It was three miles of gradual incline before I'd be there, so I hopped on my seat to begin the journey. About a mile along my busy downtown street, I rode past the gift shop owned by a local ashram. As I glanced at all the goods in their window, I remembered that I needed a new meditation bench. The one I had was very old, and its screws had given way into the soft pine. The bench was literally on its last legs.

I don't really do formal meditation anymore. My meditation bench is kept in front of my toilet to rest my feet upon while I sit. I learned a while back that we humans evolved to relieve our bowels best from a squatting position. Having your feet raised up on a little bench allows your intestines to work the way they were designed to function. A standard meditation bench happens to be the perfect height for the job.

I won't go into the whole story, but the bench really does work. Let's just say that when John J. Crapper (no joke) designed the modern toilet in the 1850s, it was a major improvement. Up until then people tended to empty their chamber pots onto the street. Crapper revolutionized sanitation, but your intestines have suffered ever since.

I hopped off my bike and walked into the gift shop. The little bell on top of the door clanged as I entered, but the man behind the front desk didn't seem to notice me. He wasn't doing anything in particular, so I just assumed he was one of the over-meditated types I'd often met in the store. Their brains seemed to be stuck in the theta brain wave state, which is similar to the feeling you have when first waking up in the morning. It's that foggy place between the world of dreams and the world of having to get up and let the dog out. I'm pretty sure it's why they tend to wear the type of clothing they do. If you always feel like you just got out of bed, it makes sense to wear pajamas.

My guess is that this continual state of haziness is the result of more than three hours of meditation a day. Like all medications that kill pain, meditation can be used to different ends. I don't know what specific type of meditation this ashram practiced, but they seemed to have gone past using it to foster that relaxed but alert place of nonattachment. They appeared to be parked at a place down the road a bit called "too much of a good thing," which I recognize from personal experience. Like any other way, I'm sure their way has its strengths and its weaknesses. For me, they appeared a little too numb to spend a whole lot of time around, unless I was on a silent retreat—then they'd be perfect.

I wandered around the store until I found a shelf with five varieties of meditation benches on it. They were all beautifully stained and seemed well made, but since I had a nontraditional use of the bench in mind, I wanted an industrial model. I needed one that could withstand numerous daily "meditation" sessions. Basically, I wanted the bench that a three-hundred-pound meditator would purchase.

I was then struck by the fact that I don't think I've ever met a three-hundred-pound meditator. With the masses of asses in this country growing ever larger, I was quite intrigued with this realization. I began contemplating all the reasons that this might be the case when I realized I might want to seek some professional help (for the bench I was purchasing), so I walked back up to the front counter and asked if I could get some assistance.

The dark-haired man with glazed brown eyes looked up with a face completely devoid of expression. After fairly lengthy consideration, he decided that I was in fact worthy of his assistance. Of the 1,440 minutes he was allotted each twenty-four-hour day to function in the world, he had decided to spend two of them interacting with me. I couldn't help but respect his prudence, as I too realize that time is one of the few things you can never get back.

He came around the counter and began walking toward the meditation benches. I followed at the seeming funeral's pace he had set and surmised that maybe my experience was a combination of me drinking too much coffee and him being customer-service challenged. It was clear that he could never make it as a librarian, but he appeared to be physically well-bodied, so a genuine curiosity was piqued within me.

Our caravan continued as we moonwalked to the far off land of the benches. In slow motion, we alternately lifted each foot, moved it forward in midair, and then placed it on the ground. I had effectively stepped into his world for a short time and began to appreciate the unique ambiance his way of being created. Before I had *seen* each movement of the storekeeper as one small step for a man, but now I *experienced* each one as a giant leap for mankind. He must have enjoyed the feeling of historical importance that accompanied each of his body's movements. He was Neil Armstrong walking on the moon, while remaining here on earth.

He moved with such grace that it was mesmerizing. There was not an ounce of wasted movement. The storekeeper had a consistent glide that would have been the envy of any conveyor belt or Tai Chi master. Had he been in the hustled pace of what the rest of us consider normal life, he would have been run over, trampled. But he had found a way of life where he could comfortably be who he was, fully. While it wasn't quite my style, who cares if it wasn't my style, it was *his* style. And it was an impressive one.

"Are you a serious meditator?" Neil asked.

"I have used my current meditation bench every day for the last twelve years, without exception," I replied, not wanting to bore him with my John J. Crapper story.

"Who is your meditation teacher?" Neil inquired, with just a hint of ego.

I knew I was in trouble now. I wanted to maintain the moonwalk connection we'd just experienced together. It could be lost if I named the wrong teacher from the wrong school of meditation. I might even be deemed unworthy of a bench and shunned from all future capitalist exchanges with the store. So what else could I to do, but give him a little of my way, and see where it went.

"I did have a teacher," I explained, "but we got into an argument over which one of us was more serene, and she fired me as her pupil. I would rather not mention her name, but you can probably figure out who it is."

"That is unfortunate," Neil replied without the slightest inkling of amusement. "Was she local?"

I've learned to never underestimate any community's love of gossip, spiritual community or otherwise. Neil was human after all, and I could begin to sense that we might be able to reconnect through the use of my witty meditation teacher humor.

"She hasn't been around lately," I answered.

His eyes rolled up as he considered whom I might be talking about. Neil was engaged. We were having an actual conversation, but I needed to indulge his curiosity further if our little chat was going to continue.

"Let's just say it reached a point where I just felt I was way more humble than she was. She also seemed a bit pessimistic, so I knew it would never work out. I really shouldn't say much more."

"I see," he commented, with the warmth of an auditing IRS agent.

I thought the outrageously funny idea of two people arguing over who was more serene, or me taking pride in how humble I was, or my being a total pessimist about someone else's hint of pessimism would be enough to make Neil actually chuckle. It was not. I thought my humor might lighten his load, but his gravitational field was already like that of the moon. He had no desire for me to do any lightening on his behalf. He was fine just the way he was and his reply had made that clear.

The odds of him finding humor in my words were in direct correlation to the odds of me telling him I was going to put the bench in front of my toilet. Neither seemed remotely possible in the near future, so I pressed on. I asked which bench people tended to buy for meditation centers or other heavy-use locations and then made a selection. While paying at the counter and exchanging money, I refrained from joking that "change must come from within." This was done both out of respect for Neil and because I was sure it would go nowhere.

I strapped my new bench and my coffee to my bike rack and hopped on the seat. I began pedaling and shifted to a more appropriate gear to make my ride up the shallow grade a bit more manageable. Having found just the right gear, the pedaling became noticeably more fluid. Even I found it odd how much pleasure I derived from determining just the right gear for each surface I rode upon.

My joy in changing gears made me realize that, unlike me, Neil probably enjoyed the *one-gear* experience of living. Like the cruiser bikes that people ride on the paths by the beach, there is no energy wasted on shifting gears. On one of those bikes you don't even bother to climb steep hills because it just doesn't work. As long as you stay on flat terrain, then the one-gear way of living is probably a good way to go. I could appreciate that Neil had found one gear that he preferred over all others. It worked for him, and I respected that.

Neil was typical of other members of this ashram whom I'd encountered over the years who seemed to be barely tethered to the planet. They were quite nonattached to most of the happenings in life, but also very attached to being that way. They renounced everything, which is certainly one way to go, but joy often seemed to be the casualty. It's a fine line between being nonattached, but still connected, and being detached.

But that's just me looking in from the outside at the wonderful world of Neil, which is all just a big guess. The moonwalking experience I'd had with him showed me something I'd never considered about his way of being. I have no doubt that there are many other elements of Neil's way of which I'm completely unaware. Just like every person on the planet, he had an internal reality that I would never be able to experience, so what the hell do I know? Maybe on the *inside*, he really got a big kick out of my jokes. I just appreciated that he could teach me so much in the two minutes we had spent together.

With each push of a pedal the bike moved up the hill like an aging Sherpa. I had to admit that living in the flats sure would take less energy at times, but I still enjoyed the fullness of the whole up-and-down experience of varied terrains. I guess that's where Neil and I were built a bit differently. We were both lined up with life in a way that worked for us, and hopefully for those around us, which is perhaps the ultimate wisdom.

A sudden onshore breeze on my back helped the pace as I pedaled. Then the delicious smell of the warm ocean triggered a memory from when I was five years old—I was lost and disoriented on a busy summer weekend at Newport, Rhode Island's 2nd Beach. The recall began just as I had finished a deliciously crunchy peanut butter, sand, and jelly sandwich on white bread. I spotted an unclaimed yellow Tonka truck and headed toward the water's edge. That's where kids my age were doing all the serious playing.

The kid with the entire Tonka collection at his disposal didn't notice that I was operating his dump truck without authorization for quite some time. I had transported at least three full loads of sand to my own construction site before he requested his truck back. I wandered off to see what other unauthorized use of toys I could engage in and pretty quickly found one of those paddles with a little ball connected to it by an elastic band. It was abandoned on the beach with no owner in sight.

The paddle toy had been abandoned for good reason: it is the most disappointing toy ever manufactured. The goal was simply to whack the rubber ball with the paddle repeatedly as the rubber band shot the ball back at you. Although the concept was elementary, the execution was not. What the manufacturers of this horrible toy neglected to mention was that the game was virtually impossible. Even teenagers lacked the hand-eye coordination to perform more than three sequential hits with the paddle and ball, and they were much too old to ever play with such a toy.

Being young and naïve, I attempted to have some fun with the torture toy. We've all done it, so I know I'm not alone. I tried little whacks with the paddle that would send the ball up in the air four or five times without engaging the rubber band, but of course this was boring. As soon as I hit the ball harder and engaged the rubber band, I was down to one or two strikes. I tried an assortment of different techniques. Hitting the ball straight down met with no success, nor did horizontal strikes. Eventually, I determined the only winner of this game was the manufacturer who had made a buck by selling the product. Like the child before me, I abandoned the toy in the sand.

I wandered along the beach for a while longer until I realized that I needed a little pick-me-up in the form of a sugar-packed drink known as Kool-Aid. My mom didn't mess around when it came to mixing up a batch of Kool-Aid. If the instructions said to add one cup of sugar to a certain amount of water, then she added two. All she knew was that sugar made kids happy, and happy kids was the goal. Later when the sugar crash kicked in, we would be happy sleeping kids, so it was great all the way around for her.

As I began trying to locate my family's red-and-white checkered blanket, I spotted the lifeguard chair that I thought marked its location. I walked around and around the area with no luck. I then went to the next lifeguard chair and repeated the process. I did this at approximately four lifeguard stations until I realized that I was totally lost.

It was at this point that I employed the most effective strategy I could think of. I stood in place and began to cry. I looked around and cried, looked around and cried, looked some more and cried. Naturally, people in the area could sense that this was just a cry for help, so they ignored me. After all, this was the East Coast and not a place for the faint of heart.

The beach was absolutely packed. There was about two feet between each family's set of blankets, and there were probably three or four thousand separate groups of people on the beach. I wanted to be like one of those baby penguins you see on television that amongst thousands of other penguins somehow picks out its mother's unique squawk and is guided home. So I listened, but all I could hear was Smokey Robinson's "Tears of a Clown" blaring on the radio next to me. Okay, it might have been "In the Summertime" by Mungo Jerry, but that doesn't go as well with the story now, does it? I was also pretty sure my mom wasn't squawking for me anyway, so the blaring music wasn't really a factor.

Fortunately, an old man took pity on me and came to my aid. His skin was a deep brown, wrinkled type of leather I'd never seen before. Had I been to Florida where this type of skin is commonplace, I'm sure I would have been less intrigued.

"Are you lost?" he asked.

"Ye ye yesssss," I hiccupped through my tears.

"Can I help you find your parents?" he inquired.

"Okay," I whimpered.

Shady Grady was the leathery man's name, and he had apparently shown up in Newport around the time the glaciers had begun to carve out the cliffs at the south end of the beach. Like many of this type, his chosen occupation had eventually become the being of himself. It was, after all, a full-time job. His skin was the type that had been softened up during untold conversations that took place standing beside someone's beach blanket. Over the years, the ultra-violet light that was being sought out by all the visitors to the beach had gently broken down the elasticity in his tissue. The downward force of gravity had carved its reflection into his sagging skin.

This was an old man who fully embraced the freedom that came with an earth suit that had paid its dues. It had wandered around the planet for seventy or so years, and he was quite pleased with whatever abilities it had left. When he raised his arms and pointed in different directions to help me find my parents, I noticed that what used to be his triceps were now his "bingo wings" (that's what the old ladies at church called them), and they flapped in the wind with each movement of his outstretched arm. He could not have cared less. It was part of who he was, and he offered no excuses or apologies.

Shady Grady and I wandered somewhat aimlessly in search of my home blanket, but I was happy just to have an escort. After I had calmed down, I began asking him questions. "Do you work here? What's your name? Where's your wife?" to which I received all the standard answers.

"What's your job?" I asked Shady.

"I'm a water bearer," he quipped.

"What's that?"

"Well, each day I take in water and then throughout the day I carry it to different places and make small deposits," he chuckled.

"Oh," I said.

I was pretty sure he was one of those guys who delivered big water bottles to places like my dentist's office.

I don't know how long Shady Grady and I walked up and down the beach, but it was a good while. It was the third or fourth time past my family's blanket before I spotted my toy Budman (yes, Budweiser's), standing proudly on our red-and-white Coleman cooler. There's nothing quite like the representative of a beer company being marketed as a child's toy. Between Budman and the Clydesdales, my first choice in alcoholic beverages as a young adult was already made for me.

My mother's longtime childhood friend, Sister Joan, gave me Budman. She was a Catholic nun who lived and worked in "the projects" (public housing) in South Providence. To this day, Sister Joan is one of the most uplifting, light-filled human beings I've ever encountered. In her standard attire of a long skirt and work boots, she's smart enough to ignore the church when they get in the way of her helping those in need and wise enough to crack open a Budweiser at the end of a long day of service.

I'm pretty sure that no one in my family even noticed that I'd been missing when Shady Grady delivered me, as promised, to my parents. They pleasantly thanked him for my safe return and then began chatting about boring grown-up stuff. I sat happily guzzling Kool-Aid until Shady Grady bent down and looked me in the eye.

"Do you want to see how G.I. Joe would find his blanket at the beach?" he asked.

I gave an affirmative nod.

"Come with me," he said as we headed down to the water's edge.

We arrived on the wet sand and turned to face all the beach goers on their blankets.

"Can you see how all the lifeguard chairs look alike?" Shady asked.

"Yes."

"Well, you can't use only the lifeguard chairs to find your parents when you get lost, because they all look the same. Do you understand?"

I nodded.

"But if you stand right in front of your lifeguard chair," he instructed, "you can see that big flag in the parking lot right over the lifeguard's head. Now let's walk to the next one."

When we were directly in front of the next lifeguard chair, Shady's voice got a bit more serious.

"Now when you stand right in front of this lifeguard chair, can you see how the big flag in the parking lot isn't over the lifeguard's head, but that little yellow house on the hill seems to be right above his head?"

I nodded.

"Whenever you come to the beach, you can walk down to the water and see what object out in the distance is over your lifeguard's head. When you stand right in front of your lifeguard chair, only your lifeguard chair will have that one thing over his head. Understand?"

"Yes," I happily asserted.

"Most of life is just about getting your bearings. Once you're lined up, things are a lot easier," Shady Grady said, poking me in the chest with his old man fingernail to drive the point home.

"Okay," I agreed, not wanting to get poked again.

With that, Shady Grady patted my head with his leathery paw, and walked away in full confidence that I would be able to find my blanket all by myself.

Even though Shady's final point was a bit fuzzy, his teaching had opened up a whole new world for me. I began walking down the beach testing out this revolutionary way of finding your blanket. Standing in front of each lifeguard chair, I found that there was some distinct way of orienting myself.

I tried to explain the wonders of orientation to others, but didn't do it as well as Shady Grady. Most people looked at me like I was talking about hallucinations that were appearing over common objects. Both of my parents would give me the "that's very interesting" type of responses. Even as a kid I was aware that their replies were complete bullshit. But I knew it was a real thing, even if I couldn't explain it.

In my desire to avoid a repeat of being lost at the beach, orienting my location became a minor obsession. Parking lots became annoying to everyone in my company as I took a few extra seconds to get aligned. Personally, I didn't think I was asking too much. Once I noticed the chimneystack that lined up behind the big K in Kmart, the entire family was free to go. The water tower that looked like it was sitting atop the W on the Piggly Wiggly sign was more than adequate for us all to carry on with the day's business. Was this asking too much? I think not.

This way, I could always find my way back to the family car. It made my life much easier. Except for the one time I found our car after being lost in the store. The rest of the family claimed they were in the store looking for me for over an hour (I say, it was twenty-five minutes, tops). Surprisingly, water towers, street lights, flag poles, and other objects I had used to verify my bearings were always in the same place when we came out of the store as they were when we went in. I never grew tired of it.

To perfect my system, I would often venture out into the field across the street from my house, which except for the cow pies, was the perfect place to practice my astronaut-orientation exercises. I'd line up objects like Mr. Murphy's CB radio antenna with the yellow AMC Pacer in the Sullivan's driveway and the branch of the willow tree with the telephone pole. I'd then drop a penny in the field where I stood. Next, I would run at a dead sprint back to my house, touch the mailbox (this was required to make it an official experiment), and then run back to try and find my penny. It worked every time, and I think this realization of the amazing power of orientation may have tweaked my brain a bit. It may have caused me to look at people and situations from different angles to try and figure them out.

My concern with orienting myself may seem slightly obsessive to some people, but we kids were always getting lost back then. The first thing you did when you entered Kmart was declare to your mom, "I'll be in the toy section," as you dashed off into the maze of aisles. At least once each time we were in a department store, you would hear an announcement over the loudspeaker about a lost child, but it was a bit different from what you would hear today.

"We have a lost little boy," the store speakers would blare. "He's wearing a light blue shirt and blue Toughskins jeans. If you would like him back, please come to the front desk."

I always found it interesting that they gave the parents the option of picking up their kids (or not).

To this day I never lose my car in a big parking lot because I habitually orient my position. I also try to do this throughout my life. Living well is much simpler (but not always easy) when I remember Shady Grady's fingernail-jabbing advice. I just do my best to align the life I lead with who I am. It seems to work pretty well, most of the time.

Once you start to align your life with who you are, the same situation that was once difficult or unpleasant can become fascinating, joyful, or something entirely unexpected. Sigmund Freud once said, "A man should not strive to eliminate his complexes, but to get into accord with them: they are legitimately what directs his conduct in the world."

Try not to be distracted by the fact that Freud was a sexually repressed cocaine abuser who said lots of stuff that we totally disagree with; the above quote is pretty good. Or as the old psychoanalysis joke goes, "We don't want to throw out the sublimation principle with the Oedipus complex." Funny people, those psychoanalysts.

A lot of life does seem to come down to paying attention to the actuality of how you are and the consequences that arise when your way of being meets the various situations of life. Paying attention—and a little luck—may ultimately be the only ways to get into accord with ourselves. Until we get our bearings, we can spend a whole lot of time standing in the sand crying, while we wait for someone to help us. If you're fortunate, Shady Grady, Freud, or a good friend will come along and help point you in the right direction, but even then you have to be paying attention.

In the end, I guess it is a learn-as-you-go life, the lessons learned in regard to the ancient injunction "Know Thyself" being some of the most important. The learning itself can certainly be uncomfortable, even painful at times, but that does seem to be where most of life's wisdom is found. And once you've got your bearings, flexing the wisdom earned in being true to yourself can lead to some of the most fulfilling times of all—in the living of an authentic life.

Both Ends of the Stick

I continued pedaling homeward through heavy breaths and grinned as I accessed some of my genetically programmed stubbornness. It would come in handy for the conquering of the hill I was climbing. Sweat began to form on my brow as my mind dropped Freud into the mix with his statement that the Irish were a race for which psychotherapy was totally useless. I did love the statement because I always felt it was both an insult and a compliment. With some of the folks I grew up around, I can see why one might be distracted by the often-intractable nature of the Irish psyche. This may have caused Freud to miss the poetic light that lies within the heart of the Irish. A poet understands that no matter how well you "get into accord" with your complexes, life will hand you a full range of experiences. A poet, a sage, a warrior, a wise elder, embraces this understanding.

My eyes were now glued to a point five feet beyond my slowly rotating front tire. It was the present moment trance that would be required for me to get up the hill. I knew this was the inevitable balance point for the easy downhill glide I'd had earlier in the day. I didn't know the trance would transport me back to visit with a favorite wise elder from my childhood.

Ben and I were about eight years old, casting our fishing lines into the waters at the fish-barren Rough Rock Ridge, so there was plenty of time to scour the shoreline with the binoculars in hope of catching Big Foot getting a drink. Big Foot had apparently chosen a different watering hole on that day, but I did spot something just down the shoreline at Sunfish Spot.

In the shade at the water's edge, right where the reservoir narrowed, I eyed a fox. I had seen foxes before, but this one was delicately stepping backwards to submerge himself, butt first, below the water's surface. It was intriguing. At first I thought he was just a tentative swimmer, but he was going much too slow for that. And he wasn't hunting for crayfish or he'd be facing the other way. I consulted with Ben, and he concurred that something strange was happening.

Inch by slow inch, the fox backed deeper and deeper into the water. When the water reached his neck, he tilted his head back and slowly immersed his ears. Next went his eyes, until only the tip of his nose was above the water's surface. He waited a few seconds and then pulled his nose under too. He disappeared under the water for a moment and then shot out, running back into the woods.

This was strange, perhaps even undocumented animal behavior. I still had every intention of being an astronaut, but my back-up occupation was to be Marlin Perkins's assistant on the television show *Wild Kingdom*. It goes without saying that I would be the guy who wrestles the boa constrictors and tackles water buffalo, so I needed to know why a fox would do such a thing.

Much to my dismay, nobody I knew could tell me why a fox would behave in such a strange manner. Most adults thought I was making the whole thing up or that I had gotten sunstroke and imagined the entire event. Other kids, especially my sisters, just didn't seem to understand the importance of the matter and couldn't stay focused on the problem. I took it upon myself to widen my circle of expert opinion.

I needed someone who would really listen to me, but I realized it had to be someone who was closer to the elements than the average adult. It was then that I decided to seek out the expertise of Mr. Gooch.

Mr. Gooch would walk by on occasion when Ben and I were out fishing. Depending on the time of year, he'd often be carrying a rabbit, a pheasant, or a turkey that he'd caught. Whenever he walked by with what we assumed to be his dinner slung over his shoulder, Ben and I would ask him endless questions about his latest catch while we petted his black lab, Duke.

Mr. Gooch lived on the opposite shore of the reservoir in an old farmhouse. Over the years, I'd seen him getting wood for the fire or shoveling snow from his walkway when my mother and I were driving to Jesse's auto repair shop. Sometimes Jesse would let me operate the hydraulic lift by pressing the pedals with my foot. It was fun to lift the cars up and down, so I always went to Jesse's with my mom whenever I could. We would always wave to Mr. Gooch as we drove by, and he would wave back if he saw us. I just knew that he would be able to tell me what that fox was doing when he dunked himself, tai-chi style, into the water.

Ben wasn't quite as interested in the mystery of the fox, but he figured it might be cool to go see Mr. Gooch and his dog, Duke. So one muggy summer day we hopped on our bikes and rode the four miles down our country roads to Mr. Gooch's house. It was quite an adventure for a couple of eight year olds. We had brought some change so we could stop halfway at the town fire station and buy a Coke from the machine by the back door. Going to buy a Coke at the fire station was often a worthwhile venture in and of itself, so going to Mr. Gooch's was an added bonus.

We rode down Mr. Gooch's curvy dirt driveway, and Duke barked as we parked our bikes and went to knock on the front door. Mr. Gooch called out from the barn on the other side of his property. I'm pretty sure he was surprised when Ben and I came around the corner, but he greeted us cordially. He had on wire- rimmed glasses, which he didn't usually wear, and an apron to cover his red work shirt and jeans.

Mr. Gooch told us that he was working, but we were welcome to come in if we wanted to visit. We walked into his workshop and were amazed at what we saw. It was a museum as far as an eight year old was concerned. Skinned and stuffed animals that the local hunters had brought in filled the walls and shelves of the workshop. There, right before our eyes, was life and death, before and after, in a concrete, not-to-be-denied form. Some might think that this was a lot for a couple of kids to take in, yet seeing all these animals up close was too cool for us to be wigged out by the life-and-death nature of it.

Mr. Gooch picked up that I had come all the way to his home for a reason and seemed to take me quite seriously. He listened very carefully to what I had witnessed with the fox at the reservoir. (I left out the information about Big Foot. That was strictly on a need-to-know basis.) Ben was busy examining the stuffed pheasant in the window and a large-mouth bass hanging on the wall. Mr. Gooch listened patiently to all the details of my story and allowed a long pause to make sure I had finished the telling of my tale.

"Well, it sounds like your fox had a case of the fleas," he proposed with a gentle grin.

I stood and looked at Mr. Gooch in silence. When it was clear that I didn't understand, he explained further.

"As the fox slowly dips his body below the water, the fleas flee. They move up his body toward his head until they are finally left sitting on the hairless tip of his nose. Then the fox goes all the way under the water, and the fleas just float away."

"Why doesn't he just scratch them away like my dog?" I inquired.

"Because that doesn't work. Scratching only seems likes it's helping. Your dog just moves the fleas to another spot on his body."

"Oh," I murmured.

"In life," Mr. Gooch laughed, "just because you are doing something doesn't mean you're getting anything done."

"Why doesn't the fox just jump into the water all at once?" I asked.

"Because that doesn't work, either. Then the fleas just clamp down wherever they are and hold on. And fleas can hold their breath for a long time."

I stood silent.

"Sometimes in life you need patience," Mr. Gooch added. "You have to have the courage to wait because some things need time to happen. Someday, you'll understand it's just the way certain things are."

"Really?"

"Oh yes, and even then, even when you are courageous and patient, some things will never be the way you want. That's why you have to enjoy the things you can, while you can, because lots of times you don't get them back, ever."

Mom had told me Mr. Gooch's son was killed in Vietnam, so I figured he might be talking about that, but he never said for sure.

"You see, what I do here is called taxidermy. My grandfather was a taxidermist, as was my father. I've been doing this for about forty years now, but it took a lot of time to learn how to do it. As much as my father and grandfather helped me, I had to learn on my own that much of doing anything properly is knowing that you can't force things. Life's a lot about paying attention. If you pay attention, you can spend a lot more of your time doing things that will actually be effective."

I felt like I was getting a life lesson from Master Po, so I took it all in as best I could. Ben was busy touching all the glass eyeballs of the stuffed deer, raccoon, and anything else he could reach, so neither of us was too worried about him.

"Do you like bears?" Mr. Gooch asked.

"Yes," I chimed.

"Have you seen the polar bear at Slater Park Zoo?"

"Uh-huh."

"Would you like me to tell you my favorite joke?"

"Okay."

Mr. Gooch's eyes got big as he began:

A Mama polar bear and her little son were standing on the top of a snowdrift on a cold winter day up at the North Pole.

"Ma, what kind of bear am I?" the little bear asks.

"You're a polar bear, son. You know that," the mom answers.

"Oh," says the little polar bear, "but Mom, do you think that maybe I'm a grizzly bear?"

"No," says the mama bear, "you're a polar bear. We're the only bears up here at the North Pole."

"Oh," replied the little bear. "Do you think maybe, just maybe, I'm a panda bear?"

"No," says the mama bear, "why do you keep asking all these questions?" "Well," says the little bear, "because I'm cold."

I'll be honest. I didn't get it, but Mr. Gooch seemed so pleased with the joke that I found myself smiling along with him.

"Even polar bears get cold," he explained, "everyone has hard times, so you enjoy the good times when they're here, okay?"

"Okay," I agreed.

"What else are you and Ben doing this summer?" Mr. Gooch asked.

I now felt I could trust Mr. Gooch.

"Ben and I are looking for Big Foot in the woods around the reservoir and the pit," I confided.

"That's exactly what I'm talking about," Mr. Gooch said. "That sounds like great fun. I like the woods, too."

"Have you ever seen Big Foot?" I asked.

"Come to think of it, I never have."

"We look for him by the edge of the water because we figure he must get thirsty in the summer."

"That sounds pretty good to me."

"Do you think if Ben and I are patient like the fox, we'll see Big Foot?"

"I don't know, but I do know that lots of times the fun is in the doing and pursuing, not in the getting and then forgetting. I think the more you and Ben enjoy looking for Big Foot, the more successful you'll be."

"But I don't want to be like the dog scratching his fleas; I want to be like the fox," I clarified.

Mr. Gooch let out a soft chuckle and looked me directly in the eye.

"Life's not always about getting rid of the fleas. Sometimes it's about the joy found in the scratching."

"So it's both?" I asked with a lilt of confusion.

"Oh yes, life is both. The trick is knowing which is which," he said, "but you and Ben seem to be doing pretty well, so don't worry about it too much."

"'Cuz when you pick up a stick, you get both ends," I stated.

Mr. Gooch's chin pulled in toward his chest, and his eyes widened. He was impressed with my summation. I'd been previously coached on this concept, but I didn't let on.

"Exactly," he commended. "You've got it. Good for you."

There was a long pause as Ben and I missed our cue to leave.

"Okay guys, I've got to get back to work," Mr. Gooch nudged. "You can pet Duke on your way out."

Mr. Gooch never asked me about my wisdom-filled reply about picking up a stick, but heck, I'd known that since I was five. My friend Little Joe had taught me that years ago.

Little Joe was what today we'd call a "little person." Technically he had a condition known as pituitary dwarfism that left his body very small but overall proportional. Because we were much less sophisticated back then, and since Joe was little, adults and children all lovingly called him Little Joe. I never remember him being anything but absolutely delightful with all who encountered him. He was either enlightened or just didn't give a shit anymore; it's hard to tell the difference sometimes.

Little Joe was a bit more than three feet tall. His voice was a perfect match to the members of the Lollipop Guild in *The Wizard of Oz*. He always wore jeans with the legs cuffed up. And he always wore brown, lace-up shoes. Never boots. Never sneakers. He also walked everywhere he went, and the set of keys that were hooked to his belt loop always jangled as we walked next to him.

All the kids loved Little Joe. He would walk down the street, and the moms would call out to their kids, "Little Joe is walking by." We would all drop whatever we were doing and sprint out of the house to chat with Little Joe for a hundred yards or so as he passed.

Little Joe would ask us simple questions like "How are you?" and "How is school?" We, in turn, would inquire as to where he was going and why he always walked everywhere. He never seemed to tire of our incessant questions that I'm sure were repeated by kids all over town. He never slowed down his pace for us, but he also never sped up. As long as we could keep up, he seemed to enjoy the conversation.

There are some memories in life that seem to summarize the best of times; my memories of sprinting out of the house to say "Hi, Little Joe!" are just those. I vividly remember the day in my early twenties when my mom called me in California to tell me Little Joe had died. It was one of the most bittersweet moments I've ever experienced. I hadn't seen Little Joe for many years, but a movie reel of my child-hood friend played in my head. I could hear his jangling keys clipped to his belt loop and his Lollipop Guild voice answering all our questions with nothing but kindness.

"Why don't you drive a car?" I asked him one day when I was five.

"Because I'm too small to drive a car," he matter-of-factly replied.

"Does that make you sad?" I inquired, as only a child would.

"When I was young it did," he acknowledged, "but someday, when you're an old man like me, you'll know it's just the way some things are. Someday you'll understand that when you pick up a stick, you get both ends."

"What does that mean?" I asked.

Little Joe was silent for moment as he thought about my question. We kept walking at his regular pace down Scott Road until he veered to the right and picked up a small stick on Mr. Quigley's lawn. Then, for the first and only time I can ever remember, Little Joe stopped walking. He turned and faced me. He was about my height, so it was much like I was talking to one of my friends. The stick was just about as wide as his shoulders as he held it in front of me with his left hand.

"No matter where you are in life or where you want to go, there are good things and not-so-good things that come with every situation," he explained. He alternately pointed to each end of the stick as he continued. "The people in their cars get to the places they're going much faster than I do, but they don't get to meet anyone along the way. I don't get to places very fast, but I know everyone in town. Life is always both ends of the stick, never just one."

I paid close attention as he spoke. I wanted to understand what Little Joe was saying because I could tell it was important to him. He continued pointing at the two ends of the stick as he talked.

"You have to eat your vegetables, and then you get dessert. You have to do your schoolwork, and then you get recess. I have to work to make money, before I can go on vacation. Life always has two ends, like a stick."

He took a powerful pause.

"If you remember this stick it will make your life a lot easier, especially when times are hard," Little Joe continued. "Life is happy and sad. Life has pleasure and pain. It's hard to be happy if you think you can have a stick with only one end. And you can only be jealous of other people when you don't see both ends of their stick."

He stared at me with his chestnut brown eyes to make sure I understood what he was saying. When he felt that I had understood, he handed me the stick, turned, and went on his way.

Up until that moment, I had never really thought about Little Joe being an old man. Right before my five-year-old eyes, he had become a real person who had lived a life with thoughts and feelings, pains and pleasures. He was unique, just like everyone else, but he wasn't special—just like everyone else.

I got the gist of what he was saying. "The stick" might have been my very first esoteric teaching on life. It may have been the setup for my love of Master Po, who I wouldn't discover for another two years. It also prepared me for what Marlon Brando would tell me seven years later: "You're born. You die. In between, you laugh, you cry." Little Joe might have dropped the cosmic pebble that rippled out to make me who I am today.

I kept the stick Little Joe gave me for a long time. I tied a piece of string around its middle and hung it from a thumbtack on the wall next to my bed. From time to time people would ask me about it, but I would only say it was a stick Little Joe gave me. It had a sacredness that I wanted to protect, so I didn't go into detail.

As I got older, I could understand much more deeply what Little Joe was saying. That stick helped me a lot. I'd occasionally have some tough times, as all kids do, but when I would lie in bed, there would be my stick on the wall. I could think about things and poke at one end of the stick. Like a seesaw, as one end went down, I would watch the other end go up, and eventually both ends would get back to even.

The stick, for me, was the equivalent of the masterful saying that applies in all situations: "This, too, shall pass." Little Joe's stick really helped me to understand that life is the experiencing of both ends of the stick—never just one.

I loved that little stick. Then one day, in an unsentimental moment of puberty, I threw Little Joe's stick away. I still wish I hadn't. I'm sure it was a time when I wasn't well aligned with who I was, as happens to all of us.

It took a little while to get myself aligned with the mystery of life in a way that worked for me. When I did, I went outside and picked up a stick I thought Little Joe would have liked. I tied a string around it and thumbtacked it to the cork bulletin board in my office, where it still hangs today. Once in a while I plunk it with my finger as I'm walking by and pause to watch the ends bob up and down.

Dying to Live

My leg muscles now burned as I pedaled my way to the top of what seemed like the longest hill in San Diego. This was the final leg of my journey home, and it was hard going. There were moments along the way when I almost stopped and walked my bike, but I was saved each time by shifting to a lower gear. Had the hill gone on for even a hundred yards more, I would have been forced to stop because there were no new gears left for me to use.

As I caught my breath, I couldn't help but think that the hill of life can be a hell of a thing for someone if they don't have the right tools to deal with what they encounter along the way. It might seem like an odd way of whipping up a batch of instant compassion, but recognizing how a person's lack of tools leaves them stuck in their own human limitations is a perspective that tends to set me free. It allows me to stop judging or resisting the actualities of people's abilities, including my own.

Shifting my perspective on what *already is* seems to be my favorite tool in most situations. And it works pretty well, most of the time. The things themselves that affect us in this life may never change, but a new perspective on them can inform us in ways we never imagined, and set us free.

I've come to call this primary tool *perspective sampling*. It's the hammer I use for most of life's protruding nails, and it arose from one simple rule in my childhood home: *No bad attitudes at the dinner table*. In the long run, this rule may have done more for my well-being than just about anything else I can remember.

The rule was a stroke of genius on my dad's part. It helped make dinners a pleasant affair for all the diners at our table. Naturally, the rules didn't apply to either parent, but apart from the frustration of at least one of the five children spilling their milk every single night while we ate, my folks were generally in pretty good spirits.

For Dad, subjecting others to your bad attitude was no different than subjecting others to your body odor. It was unnecessary. Maybe it's because he climbed telephone poles all day at work in the wide-ranging New England weather patterns. I'm sure he figured that if he could be up on a telephone pole in subzero temperatures or in ninety-five degree heat without bitching and moaning about it, then his kids could manage to get through dinner with a decent attitude.

My dad's rule was not that you couldn't have a bad attitude. You were welcome to it; you just didn't get to have it at the dinner table. You were free to go to your bedroom and have a terrible time with yourself if you wanted to, but that also meant you didn't get to eat dinner or anything else that evening. However, the next morning you were perfectly welcome to eat your fill.

This simple rule made each child seriously consider if their bad attitude was worth the price of suffering through a moderate hunger strike. Don't get me wrong; sometimes it was worth it. Like the time when I was six and was unjustly punished for a minor crime I didn't commit. I had a bad attitude and stuck to my guns. I went to bed hungry that night and never regretted it.

Yet I learned that most of the time a hunger strike was unwarranted. If you were upset over a squabble with a sibling or were overruled in a negotiation regarding television, then it probably wasn't worth being hungry over. Thus, I became somewhat adept at assessing my negative emotional states and the consequences that may follow from them.

Being both blessed and cursed with a stubborn curiosity about things, along with a wit that sometimes amused others, I became slightly obsessed with learning how to shift my attitude and the attitudes of those around me. I took my findings into my public life and got pretty used to having the no bad attitudes policy as my public persona. Putting on a happy face generally made you a more enjoyable person to be around, and being who I was, I naturally applied the strategy to its extreme. Somewhere along the line I lost myself in my quest for the perpetual happy face. I began to forget Shady Grady's lesson about getting aligned with who I am, and I'd thrown out that stick Little Joe had given me. I thought the life of a one-ended stick was somehow possible.

If I had to pick the primary cause of my ill-fated attempt at one-sided living, I would have to go with the culprit known as puberty. With hair sprouting all over my body and my voice deepening, I began thinking about sex approximately every seven seconds. The internally focused sagely ways of my youth shifted to a much more externally focused way of being. My tenacious nature turned its energies toward grades, sports, and girls in that distinct and disciplined order. It was about a twelve-year haze of testosterone-induced survival-of-the-fittest behavior that allowed me to externally excel at school, athletics, and dating. And while the external success had its upside, the other end of that stick could not be denied indefinitely. Life's pendulum eventually seeks balance, so the more extreme your position on one side, the further it tends to swing to the other.

You see, I was that dog who picks up a scent and can't let it go. It's not the dog's fault. It's just the way it was bred and trained. I'd picked up the scent of financial success, and with my nose to the ground I tracked that scent over, around, or through every obstacle. I never paused along the way to get my bearings. I did not stop to ask if I actually wanted what I was chasing. I just chased the scent.

While most worthwhile journeys seem to include being lost somewhere along the way, I became disoriented to the point where I'd lost myself entirely. When life's pendulum eventually swung back in the other direction, I was forced to recall some of my most important life lessons. Oddly, these were the ones I seem to have forgotten first. The intensity of experience required to get my attention was memorable to the point that my adult life is defined by it. My life seems divided into the time before and the time after a few moments I experienced on the freeway.

I was twenty-four years old and found myself with a great job on the thirty-second floor of the Bank of Boston. With a position such as mine, certain perks were to be expected, but the one I didn't expect was the strong and persistent desire to kill myself Monday through Friday and alternating Sundays. I had enjoyed the scent of financial success. I even thrived traversing the academic terrain the chase had led me across. I just had no desire to reside in the place where all my efforts had landed me. Having lost connection with who I was, I was paralyzed when it came to choosing a direction of escape. After prolonged paralysis, the ultimate escape seemed like the only viable option.

A long chain of cause and effect had led to my being where I was, and while this is true for everyone all the time, I took it personally.

One beautiful Sunday around dusk, after an entire year of having a five-to-six-day-a-week desire to kill myself, I hopped in my car and went looking for something to drive into at a hundred miles an hour. But I couldn't find anything to hit head on. All those buckle-up, wear-your-bicycle-helmet folks had made the freeways way too safe. There were safety barriers in the way of all the stuff you could really get flattened by. The tragic ending of my life was quickly becoming a comedy. As you might imagine, it was all very depressing.

"Is there anything more pathetic than a person who fails at their own suicide?" I thought. "Really, where do you go after that?"

I decided I had better drive around a bit and think through the whole idea of suicide. I didn't want to almost commit suicide; then I'd really have to kill myself. As I was driving around contemplating the end of my life, the most interesting thoughts arose in my head. I thought of Crazy Horse before the battle of Little Big Horn saying, "Today is a good day to die," which I always thought was a pretty ballsy thing to say. Although, I did think it would have been more appropriate for General Custer to have said it, since he's the one who died that day.

"Damn, I never got to see Crazy Horse National Monument," I mused. "That would have been cool. I bet if I drove into that mountain-sized sculpture, it would be 'a good *way* to die.' Wow, anymore humor like this and I'll really have to kill myself."

The poor quality of my humor made me realize how little control I had over the ideas that popped into my head. Then I realized, once again, that none of us control the thoughts that pop into our skulls, and even the thoughts about our thoughts were not under our conscious control.

"Maybe I don't have as much control over my life as I think I do," was the next idea tossed into my consciousness for consideration. "If I could change the way I felt about things, I gladly would, but the fact of the matter is that I can't even say what my next thought will be. Nobody can."

"Where exactly is all this control I assume I have over my life? Am I somehow blind to something so obvious—my lack of control?"

I realized that I had no control over the thoughts that arose in my head, or the feelings that arose in my body, or even the interpretations of events I encountered. If I did, I would obviously have changed the ones that were making me miserable. Wouldn't everyone? That way we could all enjoy our lives more.

I had been telling myself that I should like my current job and career path, but I didn't. I laughed as I recalled that this was the same thing I was trying to tell my dad on the ride back from the zoo when I was a kid. He insisted the lady should have known not to stand so close to a polar bear. I argued that whether she *should* have known was irrelevant. The truth was that she *didn't*. It was so obvious back then.

"How could I have forgotten this?"

As has been said for thousands of years, I'd been trying to teach a pig to sing. And we all know what happens when you try to teach a pig to sing: the pig gets annoyed. This is mainly due to the fact that whether or not you think a pig should sing, pigs can't sing, don't sing, and won't sing. It's not in their nature to sing.

"It's a classic resisting of *what is*," I realized. "My nature is not that of a banker, and furthermore I'm just taking the spot of someone who genuinely wants to be one. My nature is no more that of a banker than it is one of a concert pianist, unless being tone deaf is some advantage that I'm unaware of."

"At least my humor seems to be improving," I thought. "That's a good thing. I think."

As my twenty-four-year-old self drove along, I noticed all the sand along the sides of the freeway that the highway department had laid down during the winter snowstorms. Memories of Mr. K's sweeping duty came rushing back as if they happened yesterday. There was also the memory of kissing Tina Lima behind Terri Fain's house in seventh grade, but that's not really relevant.

My thought fest continued.

"Maybe my idea of death needs to be examined. After all, my physical body is fine. It's not trying to kill me with cancer or flesh-eating bacteria. So maybe I don't need to kill my physical body after all. Maybe the thought, 'I want to die,' doesn't mean what I think it means."

Then it hit me like Master Po's bamboo staff: "Maybe I'm supposed to die, but not die physically. It could be that I've been getting the right message, but I've been interpreting it incorrectly. Perhaps a *spiritual* death is required, not a physical one. Maybe I just need to die out of all the false ideas and concepts that no longer serve me."

I recalled being in Po mode as I swept the pavement in elementary school. I could see the grains of sand tumbling over each other as I pushed them with the broom. I understood that I'm not just the guy pushing my broom around the playground of life, but I'm also the one being pushed and manipulated by an incalculable number of forces like the grains of sand coming out of that funnel at the Boston Museum of Science.

After adding up all the forces affecting my life, I realized my actual control over who and how I am was much less than I assumed. I was the grain of sand, experiencing everything that happens, as well as the one pushing the broom.

I realized, once again, that I was both.

"Oh my god, I'm bound within the chain of cause and effect like everyone and everything else. That's why people simply do what they do. Pass the jelly," I said out loud and laughed.

I was exhilarated. Seeing through my illusion of control gave me the same feeling I had at eleven years old when I realized professional wrestling was fake. I was instantly freed from buying into the drama of it all. Back then it only applied to chubby guys in colored wrestling tights. Now I could feel that freedom pulsing through my entire life. Not only did I not want to kill myself anymore, I was once again thrilled to be alive. And I really hadn't done anything. A bunch of thoughts floated through my head, and I experienced them. That was all that had happened. As a matter of fact, I realized that's all that ever happens. Thoughts, feelings, memories, experiences all arise of their own accord as we encounter life. I am the experiencing of them, and I deal with them as best I can, just like everyone else.

All my suffering had come from a lack of perspective. I saw that when my perspective was wide enough and precise enough, my suffering ended. When I had the illusion that I and others have much more control than we actually do, I suffered. When I saw through the illusion that we're in total control of who and how we are, I was free. I was at peace. I was fully alive—a blame-nobody kind of guy who still understood that actions had consequences.

"When you pick up a stick, you get both ends," came into my consciousness along with an image of Little Joe. Then Uncle Bernie popped into my head and in another stunning performance delivered his line, "You're born. You die. In between, you laugh, you cry."

"It's called life," I said aloud.

I laughed again.

Instead of dying a physical death that day on the freeway twenty years ago, I ended up having a spiritual death. It was a type of dying that actually allowed me to live. A type of dying that continues, as I "die" out of perspectives that no longer serve me. Now I ride the chain of cause and effect as best I can. I try not to resist it. I try not to be numb to it. At times I still find myself doing both. But since that day on the freeway, I continue to soak in the entire experience of living in such a way that what appears ordinary to others often seems extraordinary to me. And I no longer need to be old, bald, and Chinese to do it.

The reverie regarding my death, profound and enjoyable as it was, took a fair bit of my attention away from the present. My bike had picked up a bit too much speed as I glided the three hundred yards downhill toward my street. As I began making my final right turn, I noticed that the runoff from the morning rain had left a large patch of sand in the valley that was my intersection. It had dried in the afternoon sun and was now under my tires making it possible for them to give way as I turned. The bike and I slid sideways across the sandy street and into the path of an oncoming car. In slow motion I watched the driver's side tire crush the front tire of my bike. And in super slow motion I came to rest on my back and watched the front bumper of the car stop directly above the entire right side of my body.

The man driving the car jumped out and was relieved to discover me with only minor scrapes and bruises. He offered me a ride home, which I declined since my house was only fifty yards away. I walked home with my bike on my shoulder. I assessed the long chain of cause and effect that had led to my being where I was. And then a stunning thought arose in my mind,

"It's pretty dangerous riding a bike these days. I might need to get a helmet."

ABOUT THE AUTHOR

Gary Crowley was born in Seekonk, Massachusetts, and lived in the same blue-collar Irish Catholic home in the same child-packed neighborhood for the next eighteen years. Then he moved to California to attend Stanford, graduating with a B.A. in economics and another in political science. He now lives in Encinitas, California, which is near San Diego.

Gary is a bodyworker whose practice focuses on people with chronic structural pain. He was trained in Rolfing (also known as Structural Integration) eighteen years ago. He calls his work Functional Bodywork.

In 2006, he published the book *From Here to Here: Turning Toward Enlightenment*. Gary's website is www.garycrowley.com.

Sentient Publications, LLC publishes books on cultural creativity, experimental education, transformative spirituality, holistic health, new science, ecology, and other topics, approached from an integral viewpoint. Our authors are intensely interested in exploring the nature of life from fresh perspectives, addressing life's great questions, and fostering the full expression of the human potential. Sentient Publications' books arise from the spirit of inquiry and the richness of the inherent dialogue between writer and reader.

Our Culture Tools series is designed to give social catalyzers and cultural entrepreneurs the essential information, technology, and inspiration to forge a sustainable, creative, and compassionate world.

We are very interested in hearing from our readers. To direct suggestions or comments to us, or to be added to our mailing list, please contact:

SENTIENT PUBLICATIONS, LLC
1113 Spruce Street
Boulder, CO 80302
303-443-2188
contact@sentientpublications.com
www.sentientpublications.com